ANTONIO SANGIO

MY SOUL'S
PURPOSE

MISSIONS, LESSONS AND PAST LIVES
THROUGH HYPNOTIC REGRESSION

First Edition, 2020
Cover Design by Rob Williams
Back Cover Photo by Malena Vásquez
Interior Book Design by Antonio Revilla
Editors: Alejandra Travi Ponce, Juan Pablo León
English Language Editor: Debra Baethge

ISBN: 978-1-7359669-2-2
Edited in Perú

*To my beloved Catherine, who supported
me with unconditional love during the
process of finding my spiritual identity.
This book is for you.*

TABLE OF CONTENTS

FOREWORD

CHAPTER I THE POINT OF NO RETURN   15

César's Message

CHAPTER II PAST LIVES AND REINCARNATION   37

The Portal

Life as a Beggar

The Resting Place

Spirit Groups

The Library

Spirit Guides

Communication with a Guide

Planning for the Next Life (or Reincarnation)

Reyna and the Body Selection Before Birth

Contracts

Karma

The Spirit World

The Indigenous and the Spiritual World

CHAPTER III THE STUDY OF HYPNOSIS   67

The Patient Grandmother

What is Hypnosis?

What is the Conscious Mind?

What is the Critical Mind?

What is the Subconscious Mind?

Fear of Worms

CHAPTER IV REGRESSIVE HYPNOSIS   79

Regression to Past Lives and the Illusion of Time

The Man in the Wheelchair

What Else Can Be Achieved with Hypnosis?

Remote Viewing

The Spirit that Helped His Daughter Remember

To Young Hypnosis Practitioners and Students

CHAPTER V SPIRITS IN HYPNOSIS SESSIONS   97

What is a Lost Spirit?

How Do Spirits Manifest Themselves?

What Symptoms Can Attached Spirits Cause?

Who is Susceptible to a Spirit Attaching to Them?

How Can We Help a Lost Spirit?

The Burned Town

CHAPTER VI FORGIVNESS THERAPY   113

What is Forgiveness and How Does It Work?

The Rapist Soldier

The Unfaithful Woman and Forgiveness

CHAPTER VII WHAT IS A VOLUNTEER IN THE SPIRIT WORLD?   129

The Mayans

The Hopi Indians

Through the Use of Hypnosis

Ticket to the Spirit World

How Can Volunteers Identify with Each Other?

Can Volunteers Forget Their Purpose?

The Medium Who Did Not Want Her Gift

The Path of a Spiritual Volunteer is a Lonely One

CHAPTER VIII IDENTITY AND THE SEARCH FOR THE UNKNOWN   157

The Farmer and the Law of Balance

CHAPTER IX FAMILY AND SOCIAL ENVIRONMENT   163

Life is a Play

Planning the Lessons

CHAPTER X PREPARATION   171

Everything Was Planned

Suffering as an Amplifier of Learning

Healing Through Forgiveness

The Conscious Hypnosis Session

The Abandonment of a Mother

My Own Forgiveness

The Lessons in Common and Understanding of My Purpose

Conversation with a Grandmother Guide

An Extraterrestrial on Earth

Feeling Lost

CHAPTER XI THE POINTS OF SUPPORT AND THE EXTREME EXPERIENCES   201

  Accidents and Near-Death Experiences

  Cecile's Clinical Death

  Clinical Death in Another Life

  The Support Points

  My Aunt Sonia

  Miguel Sanchez "Lito"

  Edgar Cisneros "el moro"

CHAPTER XII THE TEACHERS   221

  The Loss of Material Goods

  My Mother-In-Law's Death

  Aurelio Mejía

  Dolores Cannon

  The Jewish Child in the Gas Chamber

  Michael Newton

  Hashtra and Her Guide

  José Luis Cabouli

  The Techniques and the Soul Map

CHAPTER XIII THE COINCIDENCES   247

  My Parents

  The English Language

  The Study of Computer Science

  The Abandoned Beggar

  The Egyptian Tarot

  My Information Technology Career

CHAPTER XIV SIGNALS AND MESSAGES   259

  Blair Styra

  Justine Alessi

  Dodris

CHAPTER XV CLOSING THE CYCLE WITH MY FATHER   269

CHAPTER XVI HYPNOSIS IN THE NEW NORMAL   273

CHAPTER XVII CONCLUSIONS AND ACKNOWLEDGEMENTS   281

FOREWORD

From a very young age, I questioned the beliefs I was taught at home and at school. My soul was troubled when religion asked me to believe blindly in things that made no sense to me. This attitude got me into more than one problem with my parents, family, teachers and friends. In my adolescence, the story did not change much. During this stage, I always felt as if I was looking for something that was impossible for me to define. And, the more I tried to understand what it was, the more my confusion and questioning of the doctrine I was being taught grew.

Through my father, who liked books on metaphysics, I was able to shed some light on what was going on inside me. Thanks to him, I was exposed to concepts that helped give more meaning to life and the lessons it entails. One of those texts that stirred me up was Brian Weiss'"Many Lives, Many Masters," about which we had several discussions. There, the author, who works as a medical psychiatrist in the United States, explained the concept of reincarnation through his experience with one of his patients, whom he called Catherine.

When I was twenty-three years old, my father left the family to form a new commitment. Not having him around when I needed his guidance and advice the most, made me feel lost and confused for a long time. So, I began an intense search for answers and healing of my emotional wounds.

It was in this period that I began to know myself, hand in hand with people I considered to have been divinely placed in my path to keep me from straying from it. It was during this time of self-discovery that I received messages from light beings, transmitted through people with psychic abilities. In this way, my spiritual awakening began; that is, understanding who I was and why I had come to this life.

It wasn't until I was in my forties that the same book by Brian Weiss would fall into my hands again, after the death of my mother-in-law. At that moment, I was able to read it in its entirety by myself, with a more open mind, and without the presence of my father. So, after finishing it, I decided to learn about hypnosis regression.

It was over the next few years that my learning and preparation slowly aligned with my purpose and mission. I had the honor of learning from great teachers, such as Dolores Cannon, Aurelio Mejía, Michael Newton - through the Newton Institute - and José Luis Cabouli. It was this knowledge that greatly influenced my practice of hypnosis and the discovery of my own style and technique.

Later, through sessions with my clients, I gained a better understanding of life, its challenges, and the emotions we all experience when facing different situations, as well as the timelessness of the soul. Life is one, but experiences occur in different bodies -past lives- bringing with them to the current body, symptoms caused by unfinished business or trauma.

This not only facilitated emotional and physical self-healing for my clients, but also for me. All of this led me to look back and to realize that everything in my life had happened as it was supposed to, as well as the fundamental role my father had played in my evolution. He helped me to understand the meaning of happiness, as well as of sadness, anger, resentment, forgiveness, and finally, of irreparable loss.

In this book I not only share the path I had to walk, but also my learning process in love and suffering; as well as the concepts and lessons I learned, which today help me to perceive life on this planet as passing through one of the many schools in the universe. Here, spirits come to learn and evolve.

Antonio Sangio

I

THE POINT OF NO RETURN

In life, there are events that mark a clear before and after. I am referring to that point at which we know that things will change forever, that we will never be the same again and that, very probably, we will not continue to do the same things either. In my life, this point occurred during the visit of Aurelio Mejía, who in my opinion, is one of the best exponents of regressive and spiritual hypnosis in the Spanish language.

It was April of 2015, and this Colombian hypnotherapist, one of my four teachers in the field of hypnosis, had left almost a week before to go to Connecticut, USA, to continue his tour. There were very few who could obtain an appointment for a session with him in his busy schedule. I, meanwhile, was still recovering from an intense week of training with him. I had attended the training with my friend and colleague, Genoveva Calleja, whom I had invited to my home in Charlotte, North Carolina, for that purpose. It had been a week of much learning and sharing of experiences in the field of hypnosis, a week in which we facilitated thirty-eight sessions in six days, each lasting two hours or more.

By this time, I had been practicing the Quantum Healing Hypnosis Technique, also known in the United States as Quantum Healing Hypnosis Technique (QHHT), created by Dolores Cannon, my other teacher in the field. However, despite my experience, I had never had the opportunity to facilitate as many sessions per day as I had with Aurelio. The videos on his YouTube channel and his long list of followers on social media, caused the available sessions to attend with him to quickly fill up once he announced the country and city he would be visiting.

It was an incredible week, where I was able to witness amazing events during the sessions. In those days, I was lucky enough to have Aurelio staying at my house, meeting with his clients in my own office. This allowed me to ask him many questions I had about the subject. Not only that, but I also managed to analyze the sessions and ask him why he had chosen this or that technique. In short, I think that any hypnosis practitioner would have been envious of me when seeing the privileged position I was in.

From the moment Aurelio confirmed his visit to Charlotte, I knew deep inside that my technique and view of hypnosis as a healing tool would change. But I never imagined the extent to which this experience would transform not only my practice and the type of clients who would begin to come to me, but also my life, my wife's, and my children's.

During the days after his departure, and thanks to the videos in which Aurelio introduced me as his colleague in North Carolina, several people began to contact me. They were looking for an experience with Introspective Hypnosis, the technique he usually practices.

Another factor that contributed to the increase in calls was that he added both me and Genoveva to his list of recommended hypnotherapists on his website. Because of this, I was contacted by a woman from a city located a four-hour drive from Charlotte, who was interested in a session for one of her daughters, her niece, and a friend. Since they were coming from far away, they wanted to have the hypnosis sessions the same day, one after the other.

That would be the first time I would apply all of Aurelio's teachings in one session. It would also be the first time I would do three consecutive sessions. Not only did I feel pressure knowing that they were coming from far away, but also because I would be using this technique alone.

Most of the client names that I will use in this book have been changed to protect their identity. Only a few gave me permission to use their real names. All of the conversations during the hypnosis trances I will present are true and have been transcribed as they occurred.

César's Message

They arrived on an early Saturday morning. As usual in these cases, before the session, we had a talk about the myths of hypnosis in order to rid them of any doubts they had about the process. The idea is always to establish a relationship of trust with the client. At the same time, in that moment, it is important to break any pre-established concept that they had about this psychological therapy.

After almost three hours, the first session was over and it was María's turn. Born in Central America, this young woman had been brought to my office by her aunt. During the initial interview, in which personal information and points to work on during the session were gathered, I noticed her nervousness, perhaps because this was a new experience for her. I also observed her look, which reflected sadness caused by the situations that she had had to go through since she was a child.

Her mother had treated her and her brother very badly throughout their childhood. Until that day, María had not been able to understand the reason for her mother's horrendous behavior. We talked for almost an hour, and when I determined that we were ready to begin, I asked her to lie down on the bed in the office and begin the hypnotic induction.

Since not everyone goes into a trance the same way - as any hypnotist or hypnotherapist knows well - I decided to go with my intuition. I chose to use point in hand induction and, in a short time, María found herself in a deep trance, which allowed us to start working on her childhood memories.

Because her head and eyelids were moving rapidly, a clear indication of a deep trance, I knew she was vividly reviewing a memory, as if she were right there. Her subconscious had led her to a moment in the past, which she quickly began to describe to me. It was daytime and she was with her mother and a girl who worked for her. As she described to me what she was experiencing, her breathing accelerated and the movement of her head became faster. This was certainly a transcendental and somewhat traumatic event.

In that memory, her mother had grabbed her by the hair and was hitting her hard. María said that while her mother was hurting her, other people had come to her aid. In the midst of the trance, tears began to flow from her eyes until she could not take it anymore and broke into tears. At that moment, I decided to use the role-change technique, with which I try to establish communication with the consciousness of an absent person, in this case, that of her mother.

Although there are times when this method works only as a mental exercise, there are many others when it is possible to establish real communication with the other individual. When I reached the count of three and touched María's forehead, the tone of her voice and facial expression changed dramatically. I understood that I was communicating with the mother's Higher Self and part of her consciousness. Every person in a trance is a potential medium, and in that moment, I felt that I was really initiating a dialogue with her mother. When I asked her what was going on and why she was hitting María, her answer was simple and direct: "Because I hate her, and not just her, but her brother as well."

As the conversation continued, she told me that she hated them because their father had abandoned her. After these words, I tried to employ forgiveness therapy, but what would happen next would change forever my view of life and my practice of hypnosis.

As I continued to speak with the mother's supposedly higher consciousness, María abruptly interrupted me to tell me that her right foot was hurting. It was a discomfort that had not manifested itself to me during the interview, nor at the beginning of the session. Nor had I seen her limp when she came into my office. Because of the several sessions I had facilitated with Aurelio, I suspected that it might be an energy attached to her energetic body. In other words, a parasite or lost soul.

Below, I will share excerpts from the dialogue:

María: My foot hurts.

Antonio: Does your foot hurt?

M: Yes, my right foot hurts.

A: Okay, I'm going to take the energy from your right foot and we are going to let it express itself through you. I'm taking it. I'm taking it to your mind - I touched her forehead-. Brother, you can now express yourself. How long have you been with María? A long time or a short time?

Lost Soul: A long time.

I had managed to make contact with that lost spirit that had manifested itself as a pain in her foot. Now I had to find out why it was stuck with her.

A: I understand. And what happened, brother, why are you with her?

LS: I don't know.

A: Are you lost?

LS: I think so.

A: And what was your name, brother? Were you a man or a woman?

LS: I don't know what I am.

A: That's okay, no problem. You're spirit, you're energy. Can you tell me what happened to you? How did you get to the spiritual plane? How did your body die?

LS: I was killed!

He told me that some men had killed him, but he didn't know the reason why. So, I asked him what part of his body hurt when he was killed. Finding this out was essential to know if that ailment was being transmitted to María.

LS: The foot and the heart.

A: Is there anything that you caused to María voluntarily or involuntarily?

LS: Many problems.

A: Like what?

LS: Not being happy. I don't want her to be happy, because I wasn't happy.

After a few more minutes of conversation in which I tried to find out why he was with María and what symptoms he had caused her, the spirit told me:

LS: I want to meet Doña Carmen.

A: The mother or the aunt?

LS: No, the aunt. I need to meet her.

A: Is it the aunt who is sitting outside?

LS: Yes, that's her.

Carmen was María's aunt who had brought her. Her daughter and a friend were waiting in the waiting room as the session progressed. I asked the spirit to wait for me for a few seconds while I went to get her.

Once I brought Carmen into my office, I explained to her what was happening and why I had called her. I told her that a spiritual brother - that's what I call all spirits who are stuck or lost - was attached to María. I also gave her all the information he had provided.

One thing I realized months after that session, as I analyzed it for my own learning, was the fact that two of the three spirits attached to María were communicating with me at the same time. That's why some of the answers to my questions didn't make sense.

Minutes later, the third spirit would manifest himself by clearing up these doubts, but I will leave that part for later.

LS: Are you Carmen?

Carmen: Yes.

LS: I wanted to meet you.

C: Meet me?

A: Can you explain why?

LS: Hold my hand!

Carmen took his hand, and the spirit, through María, began to breathe fast.

LS: Thank you for being here.

A: Brother, we are here to help you. What can we do for you?

LS: I need to leave your niece alone - he answered as she breathed heavily and cried.

C: Can you tell me who you are?

LS: Raúl -he said with an energetic tone- as he extended his hand.

C: Raúl who?

LS: Thank you for holding my hand.

A: What is your relationship with María or Carmen?

LS: With María, I possessed her - he said as he moved his head from one side to the other.

A: Why do you need Carmen if your problem is with María?

LS: I love Carmen very much. I needed to get to know her through María.

Thus, we continued the dialogue for a few more minutes, while trying to put the pieces together and figure out the story behind this.

In the sessions I witnessed during Aurelio's stay, I saw how he handled this kind of situation, the questions he asked the spirits, and on some occasions, he had even allowed me to ask them a few questions as well. But this was the first time that I was faced with such a circumstance alone.

Many may think that at that moment, fear enveloped both Carmen and me, but the truth is that I was surprised at how calm I felt while conducting the session. I knew that behind this spirit attached to María, there was a being that needed help. Little by little we would be able to decipher this riddle.

LS: I feel like she was my wife. Carmen smiled nervously.

A: I am going to count to three, and when I reach three, I want you to go to another life where you can find out about your relationship with Carmen.

When I got to three, I touched her forehead. I asked him to place himself in a life where he would have been with Carmen. This was only possible if they met in a past life. The spirit, using María's body, began to move her head from side to side. The eyelids moved as if she was looking for something in time and space.

LS: I have two children -he said as she raised her hand showing two fingers.

A: Two children in that life. Were you a man or a woman?

LS: I am Carmen's husband.

A: And what was your name in that life, brother? Was it Raúl?

LS: No, César, César! he repeated, raising his voice and raising the hand Carmen was still holding. I am her husband, Carmen's husband - who would have a different name in that life - where are my children?

A: César, I'm going to explain to you what's going on.

LS: I was killed! -he interrupted, raising his hand again.

A: That was in another life -I answered-. Were you happy with Carmen?

LS: Yes.

A: What were your children's names?

LS: Juan and Rosa.

I continued to ask more questions, trying to get more information about the life where that spirit, whose name was César and had been Carmen's husband, María's aunt in her current life.

Little by little, everything was making sense. For now, we knew that César had attached himself to Maria in order to get to Carmen. Meanwhile, she was shedding tears and shaking her head at the story that was coming from her niece's lips.

A: Were you happy with Carmen?

LS: I loved her very much. Through her niece, I found her again.

I asked Carmen if she understood what was happening. With a nervous smile, she answered yes.

LS: I need to get out of here. I don't want to make María unhappy anymore. I need to let her go.

A: It's okay. I'm going to help you in that process, but we need to know what happened, is that okay?

LS: Okay.

A: You were killed in that life. Do you know why you were killed?

LS: Mistakenly. I was killed by some bad men.

A: Do you forgive those ignorant men who killed your body thinking they were killing your spirit?

LS: Yes, he replied with an agitated breath and shaking his head.

This is how we started to work together in forgiveness therapy. The goal was to help him get rid of all those negative feelings and emotions. César thanked us for being with him, while Carmen cried without letting go of his hand. She did so throughout the process.

During the course of forgiveness therapy, it is also important that the spirit apologizes to the person to whom it was attached, for symptoms caused voluntarily or involuntarily.

A: So, do you want to apologize to María for the discomfort you have caused her?

LS: No, not to her. To Carmen. Forgive me! You don't know, they killed me! Forgive me, please - she was still holding his hand.

A: She never knew what had happened?

LS: No, she thought I had abandoned her. They killed me -he said to Carmen, waving the hand she was holding. Please forgive me.

I looked at Carmen, who was totally confused. She obviously had no conscious memory of that life in which she had been married to Cesar, but he needed her forgiveness in order to leave quietly. He had to go to the light, heaven, source, or whatever name he wanted to give it.

Looking at Carmen, I waved and nodded to her, asking her to continue the conversation, as if she understood one hundred percent of what he was saying. Actually, I think that although Carmen was not aware of this, on a subconscious level there was something being worked on that would also help her in some way.

LS: She thought I had abandoned her and her children.

C: Don't worry.

LS: Please forgive me. I need to get out of here. I don't want to hurt her anymore.

C: Don't worry, stay calm.

LS: Please forgive me. I have loved you very much - she kept saying, as she turned her head towards her despite having her eyes closed.

C: Don't worry, I forgive you -responded Carmen in tears.

We had gathered all the pieces of the puzzle. We discovered that Cesar had joined María for the sole purpose of asking Carmen for forgiveness. For the spirit there is no time or space, for the spirit there is only now, and although this event took place many lives or years ago, for César this had just happened. Knowing that his wife in that life thought he had abandoned his family did not allow him to go to the light.

Once forgiveness was worked out, César was able to apologize to María for all the physical, emotional and other problems he had unintentionally caused her. After she forgave him, I asked César to begin removing all the discomforts from her body to let it heal. He agreed without any problem, but first he warned me:

> **LS**: It's not just me. There is another person here too. I can help you with pleasure.

> **A**: Then, brother, I ask you to wait for me there for a moment. Let's go talk to that other person, with the promise that you will continue to help me later. Is that okay?

> **LS**: Okay.

> **A**: Tell me where this person is located.

> **LS**: Always on the right foot - he told me by raising his index finger.

> **A**: I'm going to take that energy - I told him, putting my hand on that foot-. I am taking it to your head -and touching her forehead-. Brother, you can express yourself now. How long have you been with María?

> **LS**: A long, long time -he answered, moving her head from one side to the other.

> **A**: When you had a body, were you a man or a woman?

> **LS**: I was a woman.

> **A**: What was your name?

> **LS**: I don't remember.

> **A**: Why are you with María?

> **LS**: I've always been inside her.

> **A**: Why? What were you looking for in her?

> **LS**: I possessed her.

> **A**: Yes, but we know that possession doesn't exist. The body is María's, you've only attached yourself to her energy and that's

what you're living off of.

LS: Yes -she said, nodding her head-, and I want to continue living here.

A: Where did you meet María? How did you get attached to her?

LS: At a wake.

A: At whose wake?

LS: At mine -she answered, holding her hand to her chest.

A: So, she went your wake to mourn your departure and you took advantage and attached to her.

LS: Yes.

A: What are people going to say? That it's better not to go to the wakes because the dead will attach to us. That's not right, is it?

LS: No.

Now, while César was waiting, I had to find out the story of this other spirit and why she had joined María. I began by asking it about what was keeping her from going into the light. Should she forgive anyone? Should she be forgiven? I asked her if anyone had done anything to her or if she had any unfinished business. She said yes. Her mother, named Joan, had been mean to her.

What I would learn later on, over the course of months working with lost spirits, is that they too can attach to a person they identify with, whether they have the same likes, problems, or addictions. In this case, it was clear that she recognized in María the same suffering caused by the mother.

A: What did your mom do to you?

LS: She sold me.

A: How old were you when your body died?

LS: Sixteen.

A: Were you unhappy since your mom sold you?

LS: Yes.

I explained to her that we are all evolving spirits, that what her mother had done to her, had been done out of ignorance. She didn't know that she was acquiring a debt to the universe that sooner or later she would have to pay.

I also made it clear to her that, from the point of view of the spirit world, there is no right or wrong. Everything is learning. I had not yet finished telling her this when she abruptly interrupted me.

LS: I want to open my eyes and I can't! She said raising and waving her hand. I want to see my mom and I can't!

A: You can't because your mom is no longer in this plane, and this is not your body.

LS: I want to tell her that I forgive her.

A: Very good! She is spirit. She hears and from the light she will hear you. What do you want to tell her?

LS: That I forgive her.

She continued the forgiveness therapy, managing to forgive her mother. I asked her if she had caused María any discomfort. She told me that yes, she had caused her pain on the right side of her head. That was one of the symptoms Maria had mentioned to me during the interview.

A: Will you help me remove that discomfort?

LS: But I want to stay here -she answered, as if knowing that her time to leave was approaching.

A: To continue with your evolution, you not only have to forgive, but you also have to go into the light so that you can continue to learn other lessons. Are we going into the light?

LS: Yes.

María forgave this other spirit for the inconvenience it caused. Before she left, I asked her to remove all the symptoms caused. Once that was done, we said goodbye and she left for the light. After this, I made contact with César again.

A: César, we are ready, brother. Please, let's take away all those negative energies. Go through this body and cover it with white light. Apply the magic balm that you and I know about.

María's body began to shake, as if she had chills, and she took a deep breath. I continued to instruct her on what to do to relieve her.

Once the healing process was complete, she turned her head to Carmen, as if she could see her even though her eyes were closed.

LS: Is Carmen there?

C: Yes, I'm here, she answered.

LS: I'm out of here. Thank you. I'll leave your niece alone.

When Carmen saw that César's, spirit was about to leave, she turned around and gave me a sign by taking her hand to her chest. She was referring to one of the symptoms Maria had mentioned during the interview, that of a lump or a kind of bone protruding from that area.

A: César, before you leave, can you see what is swelling in her chest? Was it caused by you?

LS: Where?

A: Here -I answered by touching with my index finger the place where María had the lump-. Do you see anything here?

LS: That has nothing to do with me. That's her mother's - he said extending her hand with an expression of displeasure.

A: Her mother?

LS: Yes, María's mother. No, no, no, no... that's from her mom. Leave me alone.

A: Okay, I'll leave you alone. There's no problem.

After he gave us that information, I asked him to leave the body through the top of her head. I thanked him for his help and wished him universal peace.

María took a deep breath of relief. Now that Caesar had departed, I asked her to cover her body with a bright white light. As she did so, I instructed her to focus on the lump on her chest, to observe it with her spiritual eyes, so to speak, and thus help her visualize what I was asking of her.

She told me she saw a bone and felt something horrendous. Her head began to move back and forth and her facial expression showed discomfort. As she was shaking and breathing heavily, I explained to her that I would take the energy from her chest and bring it to her head, so as to let it express itself. I did this with the intention that she would be able to better understand what was happening and channel a possibly attached spirit.

I will talk about this third spirit attached to María later, when I explain the importance of forgiveness for our spiritual evolution.

After sending that spirit into the light, the session continued for about thirty more minutes. We were able to find the origin of her claustrophobia, her fear of darkness, and worms. All those traumas and fears had been generated during her childhood, as a consequence of everything that her mother put her and her brother through as revenge on their father.

Many other things happened during María's session, things that at that time were difficult to understand because they went beyond any concept, experience, and studies I had. Later I would understand better what had happened, as that would not be the only time I would help lost spirits attached to my clients.

Another incredible event of that day was being able to communicate with part of the consciousness of the father and mother - still alive - through María. This was not something I intentionally sought, as I had not mastered that concept yet. Later, with more experience gained, I would understand that we are all connected and that when we go into a trance, we come into an expanded state of consciousness. There it is possible to communicate with part of the higher consciousness or Higher Self of other people.

During that session, María's father came forward to tell her that she should forgive her mother and to please forgive him for not knowing what was happening. On the other hand, the mother told her how much she hated her, her brother, and the paternal grandparents for having assisted them with so much love.

When we finished the session, María could not remember anything. She had lost track of time while in an expanded state of consciousness. When I took her out of that trance, she looked confused, as if she didn't understand what had just happened. I don't blame her. Both Carmen and I had witnessed something that may be unbelievable to many: communication with three spirits that had been attached to her body.

That experience would forever transform my practice of hypnosis and my approach to the sessions. Until that day, I had only used hypnosis for past life regressions. My intention had always been to help people understand why they were facing such and such a circumstance in life, being clear that many lessons we must experience in this life are pending lessons that were not learned in a previous one. I had also employed regression to past lives to help understand the relationship with other people present in their current life, and thus know what to work on. Basically, I had used it to help people in the process of their spiritual awakening, but this session had been different.

With Aurelio, I had learned a different technique that included past life regression as one of the many tools used in it. For him, the focus had to be on those unfinished bits of business in this life: fears, sadness, phobias, grief, detachment, and a wide range of psychosomatic symptoms. That is, symptoms caused by repressed emotions from this life or past ones.

As José Luis Cabouli, a past life therapist from whom I learned the technique called Past Life Therapy (TVP) in the year 2020 said: running into a past life during a session is the result of therapeutic work while working on our clients' symptoms. Running into a past life during a session is the result of therapeutic work while working on our clients' symptoms. This means that our attention must be on the symptoms that are present in their current body, here and now. Later, these will be the thread to that experience, or past life, where they originated, where the person has some pending or unfinished business.

I remember that night, after the session with María, it was very difficult for me to fall asleep. My mind was trying to recreate with images all the details of that amazing session, as if it were a movie that was repeating over and over again. During those sleepless hours I was trying to understand why a human being has to suffer so much in the name of a supposed spiritual evolution. This would be the beginning of a long process. This was also a time of personal exploration, in which I would finally understand that nothing happens to us by chance.

A week later, Carmen returned to my office with other family members for their hypnosis sessions. When I asked her about her niece, she told me that she was a different person, that even the expression on her face had changed. She told me that people were coming up to her to talk. Her energy had been transformed and so had her vibration. Now, the frequency she was emitting was higher and others were noticing.

But that session had not only been a significant event for her. After that day, I began to identify myself more with what I was doing. I had always felt the desire to help others. At various stages in my life,

I looked for different ways to do this, but this time I felt that I had really found my mission.

I understood that my job was not only to help my clients - reincarnated spirits - but also the disincarnated ones. I also discovered that behind every attached spirit -lost or parasite, as some call them- there was a story, a reason why they were there. If their purpose was not to give a message or end some unfinished business with my client, they were simply there because they were lost, confused, or afraid to go into the light. Many were afraid to face the consequences of their actions, when in fact, in the light, everything is love and there is no judgment; others were waiting for a family member to cross over together.

From that day on, the type of clients that started coming to me was totally different, as were the reasons why they wanted a session. They were not interested in finding out about their past lives. Some of the people who were looking for this type of session didn't even believe in them or knew very little about it. All they wanted was to find physical, spiritual or emotional relief. They had to deal with symptoms they thought originated in this life, when they didn't necessarily.

In the days following the session with María, I began a retrospection. I went back in time and analyzed every major event I had experienced, as if reflecting on my path to the practice of regressive hypnosis. I realized that nothing I had experienced, good or bad, had been by chance. All the difficult and painful moments I went through were a preparation for the mission I would have: to help those in need, to give them a message of love, of hope, of compassion, to help them understand that we are all students of a school called Earth, that we are a classroom, a group of spirits that reincarnate from life to life in the process of our spiritual evolution, that nobody is a victim in this life, that what we have lived or are living is simply because we planned all those lessons before we were born.

The last-mentioned would be one of the most complex concepts to understand, that it is our own spirit that carefully plans what we must face and feel once reincarnated. If this time we feel in the role of a victim, it is more than certain that it is because we were a victimizer before, and now it is simply our turn to feel in our own flesh what we made others feel. This is what is known as karma, or the law of balance.

During that retrospection, I remembered an anecdote with Miguel Sánchez, or Lito, as his friends call him, including my parents and uncles. I was 23 years old when I met him, and at that age, I did not have a very clear understanding of what he used to do outside of his working hours. Now, I can say that Lito was a kind of spiritual coach, an earthly guide. The first time I sought him out was when I was going through a difficult time and I desperately wanted answers. Lito used the Egyptian tarot in a therapeutic way, as an instrument to channel information, as a spiritual x-ray to guide and advise.

That day, the first thing Lito told me during my tarot reading was that I had come to this reincarnation with a specific purpose. I remember that, surprised, he called his wife to also see what the cards showed. At that time, none of it made sense to me. My mind was too focused on other issues.

Over the years, the universe would put other people, other guides, other points of support, in my path. They would, in a way, keep me from straying from the path I was supposed to walk. Today I understand that even they did not realize what they were doing and how they were helping me to get where I needed to be. It wasn't until 2018 that, thanks to social media, I was able to locate each one of them and tell them what I was doing now. I was able to thank them for their guidance and words of encouragement. Not surprisingly, some of them did not even understand the effect they had had on me.

Today, when I talk to Lito, I can identify with him a lot. I see him as a kind of spiritual volunteer who, like all volunteers, may not be understood by others. I also consider myself one of the many who came before me, of the many who are on this planet at this moment, and of the many who will come in the future in order to raise the level of consciousness of human beings.

It is possible that several people may consider it to be my madness or that all this is a product of my mind and imagination. In any case, my intention is not to convince or indoctrinate anyone, it is to share my experience, my reality, what has worked for me, and for the people who have had sessions with me.

If everything I share in this book is in my mind, then it means that it is part of my subconscious. And, if it is in my subconscious, then it is part of my reality, the way I see the world. This is just one way of understanding how life works for me and what my soul needs to continue on this journey of learning. And, let me tell you, I am not alone in sharing that vision. There are thousands, if not millions of us.

Milton Erickson (1901 - 1980), American psychologist and hypnotherapist, believed that human beings do not relate to the world through the senses, but through internal maps, through associations created in our subconscious mind. It is for this reason that there are no right or wrong behaviors, since we only react to different contexts.

Now I understand that we have come to Earth to learn what love, forgiveness, and detachment are. Life is nothing but a theater play made to measure for our spiritual evolution. We are an actor in the play, and not the character that we have to represent. We must remember that we are a spirit having a human experience.

In the course of this book, I will try to explain the unexplainable through my experiences, those of my clients, and anyone who came to me for help. Although the truth is that they ended up helping me to have a better understanding of who I am and what I am here for. So, through their life stories, I healed my own.

PAST LIVES AND REINCARNATION

The word reincarnation is derived from Latin and literally means "to enter the flesh again". This philosophical and religious concept holds that a being begins a new life in another physical body after each biological death, and is the fundamental principle of several Hindu religions, such as Buddhism, Hinduism, Jainism and Sikhism.

The term was even used in several ancient cultures, such as ancient Greece. Pythagoras, Socrates and Plato believed in rebirth, while Egyptians spoke of transmigration of the soul; that is, the passage of the soul from one body to another.

The subject of reincarnation is one of those that have intrigued human beings since the beginning of times. Catholic and Christian religions speak openly of resurrection, but it is more difficult -but not impossible- to find passages touching this spiritual concept. In the bible, for example, one can find verses that give a glimpse of this thought.

Mathew 17:10-13

[10] *The disciples asked him, "Why then do the teachers of the law say that Elijah must come first?"*

[11] *Jesus replied, "To be sure, Elijah comes and will restore all things.*

[12] *But I tell you, Elijah has already come, and they did not recognize him, but have done to him everything they wished. In the same way the Son of Man is going to suffer at their hands."*

[13] *Then the disciples understood that he was talking to them about John the Baptist.*

In the fifth century, Adamantius Origin (184 A.D. - 253 A.D.), an influential Christian theologian, included Gnostic teachings in his writings despite his support for the Orthodox Church.

Among his main dogmas was that of the pre-existence of souls, in which he maintained that God created a vast number of "spiritual intelligences" before conceiving the material world. When God gave origin to the Earth, these preexisting disembodied souls incarnated. Adamantius was also a fervent believer in free will and opposed the idea of choice, which in Christianity consists of God choosing a person or group of people for a task or relationship.

It was not until 1857, when Allan Kardec (1804 - 1869), professor, philosopher and promoter of the doctrine of Spiritism, published "The Book of the Spirits," that the term reincarnation had a greater exposure. Convinced of a spiritual dimension inhabited by immortal souls, Kardec analyzed a collection of psychographic writings facilitated by friends and known mediums, who acted as intermediaries between the spiritual and physical worlds. It was the first time a group of scholars were heard to defend the idea of reincarnation.

For my part, I have decided to briefly talk about its meaning and origin. I don't intend to go into too much detail since other psychiatrists, hypnotists, and hypnotherapists have already provided us with excellent material on the subject. Among them are the books published by Brian Weiss, Dolores Cannon, Michael Newton and José Luis Cabouli.

But why should we be interested in knowing that we will return in another body? The truth is that once we understand how reincarnation works and its purpose, we begin a spiritual awakening and the breaking down of old beliefs. This path drives human beings to take responsibility for their actions, to forgive, to remove any feeling of victimization, to vibrate in the frequency of love, and to understand that everything in this life is learning.

In simple terms, understanding reincarnation and spirituality makes us change from the role of the passenger to that of the driver. We alone are masters of our destiny.

Perhaps, many of those who grew up under a religion, whatever it may be, and as it happened to me, will see the structure on which they built their lives shatter. I've been there myself. I witnessed a reaction of rejection in close family members and I accept that. In order to avoid overload, the first defense mechanism of the conscious brain is denial. Therefore, it is important to read this book with an open mind.

What is the purpose of reincarnation? Life on this planet is complicated enough already. Why return again and again to experience it? This is a difficult concept to understand. Even to this day, I find it hard to listen to the pains and sorrows that my clients have had to go through. Today, after dedicating myself to regressive hypnosis for a few years, I can say with certainty that the reason for reincarnation is clearly our spiritual evolution.

The Earth is one of the many schools in the universe. That's right, we not only reincarnated on this planet, but on many others. It is said that this is one of the most laborious parts of this task, and not only because the third dimension in which we live is very dense. But also because we come to experience something that we cannot in the form of spirits: emotions. These are what make life here so challenging.

One of the many particularities of this school is that it erases our memory at birth. It is not allowed to remember our past lives, because it would be like taking an exam already knowing all the answers.

But perhaps I am getting ahead of myself by talking about this journey without enumerating the concepts that a spirit encounters once its physical body dies. Below, I will give a brief description to facilitate your understanding, but, as I said above, there are other books that offer more details. What I will explain next is what I have been able to observe and verify through the sessions I have facilitated.

What happens when our physical body dies? When the physical body dies, the spirit leaves it, and is received and assisted by other spirits designated for this function. These may be our spirit guides - also called guardian angels - or deceased family members. Their purpose is to lead us into the light.

The spirit who has just disincarnated is often confused and even more so if his death was traumatic or if he was unable to realize that his physical body died. Such is the case of death in an operating room under general anesthesia, drug overdose, and of all those situations in which the person is unconscious. The mission of the spirits that come for us is to assist and provide comfort during that moment.

Many of my clients, when passing through the scene of death in a previous life, describe that spirit as a very intense and beautiful white light, but one that does not blind them. They describe that flash as a true transmitter of deep love, which often moves them to tears.

What they experience afterwards is a feeling of lightness and elevation. Several can describe their body lying down there, as well as everything that is happening around it. They can feel and know what the people they leave behind are thinking. Moreover, they try to communicate with their loved ones to explain that they are well, but the sadness in which they are immersed does not allow them to hear.

After that, they feel that they are rising through the clouds, moving away from the planet as they travel to another dimension. If you are interested in this process, you can find it very well explained in" Destiny of the Souls,"by the American hypnotherapist Michael Newton, and in"Nosso Lar" (Our home), a book channeled by the Brazilian medium Francisco de Paula Cândido (1910 - 2002), better known as Chico Xavier.

The Portal

Once the spirit is out of the body, it begins its ascent, which can occur in two ways depending on the evolutionary level and number of reincarnations it has had. When it comes to more evolved spirits, they do not see other spirits coming for them, as they already know the way. On the contrary, if you don't have much experience, you will need the assistance of other spirits to change dimensions.

Regardless of the evolutionary level, my clients have remembered entering a portal into a city of sorts. There, several lights (spirits) were waiting to receive them. Although there are variations in the description, they all report basically the same thing.

Life as a Beggar

To reinforce this information, I will share what Sabrina, for whom I facilitated a session with Michael Newton's method, Life Between Lives, reported once her body died. That past reincarnation was very hard, as it was a homeless man named Raymond who ended up being beaten to death by some young people.

Antonio: Now that you have left the body and you are floating, where are you in relation to your body?

Raymond: About him.

A: Is there anyone near that body?

R: He's been left alone.

A: If you look around, what do you see?

R: The assailants escaping onto a busy street with a lot of traffic.

A: Raymond, what do you think about the life you just lived?

R: Why did I have to live such a sad life and death?

At this point, Raymond reported a light coming for him.

A: And as you see that light, what is happening?

R: I am standing in front of a building -he answered surprised- it has colored windows, as if they are made of glass. It seems to be made of concrete, like a very old construction. They are indicating to me to go up the steps.

A: As you climb the steps, can you tell me if your guide is around?

R: Yes, he smiles. He's waiting at the door.

A: Can you describe him?

R: He has a white and gold robe, like brown with gold. His hair is long and white.

In the same way, many describe the entrance to the spiritual world. The characteristics coincide with those found by Michael Newton in his sessions and with those provided in "Nosso Lar," where the spirit of the doctor who dictated the book details the afterlife after his physical body died.

The Resting Place

Once the spirit's ascension is completed, it arrives at resting place, where spirits can replenish their energies, especially if the death has been traumatic or the agony prolonged. This site has been described several times as a beautiful garden of vivid colors. On occasion, they have seen other spirits of translucent bodies dressed in a kind of white robe or gown right there.

When they are in that place, it is difficult for them to answer questions, because in that dimension time and space do not exist.

The person in the trance is literally in the resting area and that is what they want to do. Several times I have been forced to bring them forward to the time of departure to continue the session.

To give a better example of what the spirit experiences in that space, I will share a segment from Gina's session, which took place while I was teaching Introspective Hypnosis in Peru. It is worth noting that Gina went so deep into the trance, that she didn't remember anything she talked about in that state.

Once the body died in that past life, where she was a native Indian woman, she felt that her spirit began to rise as she detached herself from the body. It is at that moment that I began to ask her what she was visualizing.

Gina: I see a lot of light.

Antonio: Come into the light. That's the source from which we all come, and tell me what you feel when you enter it.

G: I feel happy -she replied as her face showed real happiness, as if it had suddenly lit up.

A: Move to the moment you reach your destination and tell me if you see others like you.

G: It's a garden! I see people in white.

A: Do you recognize this garden? Is it a familiar place to you?

G: We come here to rest and then we study.

Gina had come to the place where she had to replenish her energy. It was flooded with much peace, silence and recollection. When I asked her what they were studying next, she said they were studying their lives, the ones that had just ended. The review is done to understand what lessons were learned and what goals were achieved in the last reincarnation.

Spirit Groups

Once you and your guide evaluate the life you have just completed or leave the rest area, it's time to meet with your spirit group or classmates, so to speak. These are made up of six to eight members, sometimes a few more.

Several of the people I have worked with have recognized the members of their group as people they have shared past lives with. These have sometimes been men, and others, women, depending on the purpose and lessons of the reincarnation.

It is common to hear the client in a trance refer to the members of their group by their spiritual name, which is not necessarily the same as the one given to the physical body. We all have one, which belongs to our eternal identity. Some spiritual names are difficult to pronounce or describe, as they may be sounds or frequencies.

Each group emanates a color. The spirit is energy and vibration, so everyone does it with a different frequency. In this aspect, I have been able to corroborate the studies of Michael Newton, who after years of investigation with his patients, was able to determine the evolution of the spirit according to the color it possessed. The base tone is a brilliant white. The more spiritual progress there is, the darker the color can become, towards yellow, light blue, and purple. There is a whole range between them. As far as I have been able to discover, purple belongs to the more evolved spirit and is usually the color of the energy of spirit guides.

The purpose of the spirit group is to help each other in the evolutionary process. Once the spirit leaves the resting place, they study a kind of book, where they find the details of all the lives they have had. The first thing they do is do a kind of evaluation to determine what lessons they should learn and what lessons are left over. Generally, they talk about forgiveness, detachment, non-judgment, love, and helping others, among other teachings.

The Library

While we are using terms that may not exist in the spirit world, both Michael Newton's patients and my own have described a place very much like a library. There you can find books or manuscripts that contain the story of our lives.

Some remember this space as a huge open room with shelves and millions of books. Others describe it more as a closed environment, similar to what we know as a library on Earth. This environment is run by a single spirit, a kind of librarian who is in charge of helping to find the required information.

Each of us has our own book with information from all our lives. This is the text that the spirits returning to the spirit world study in order to understand the goals accomplished and those pending for the next life, once their last reincarnation is over.

Some describe that, when opening the golden books, something very similar to a video in 3-D appears with everything that has been experienced. Several clients have even been able to interact with this film, as if it were virtual reality technology. Others, however, have told in sessions that the books had blank pages, whose information could only be shown to them when they were ready to see it, understand it and be able to face what happened.

It is not necessary for our spiritual guide to accompany us at this stage. They are with us from the moment we arrive at the entrance portal, during the evaluation of the last reincarnation and our entrance to the library. They are also the ones who escort us to the meeting with our spiritual group.

I will once again use Sabrina's session to explain what happens inside the library.

Sabrina had just evaluated her last reincarnation with her guide. Now, he was asking her to follow him.

Sabrina: Archie -the spiritual name of her guide- wants me to follow him. He wants to teach me something.

Antonio: And while he is telling you that, do you wish to ask him any other information about your last reincarnation?

S: He is going to teach me a book to talk about that life.

A: Follow your guide.

S: There are many books everywhere! -she said in surprise. Some are floating. He is floating and so am I.

A: What is the name of this place?

S: Akashic Records -a name also widely used, derived from the Hindu term 'akasha', which means ether or heaven.

A: Would you consider this as a kind of library?

S: Yes, a library of knowledge. All spirits come here to get information. Here they learn. Some reincarnated people come in their sleep and then come back with that knowledge.

A: I understand.

S: Other spirits come when their previous life is over to learn from what happened. It's all about evolving spirits. There are other seasons, and this is one of them.

A: Is there anyone else in that library?

S: Yes, there are other spirits looking at books. They have their guides with them.

A: Is there anyone in charge of this place?

S: Yes, he wears a red robe. He looks as if he's at some kind of desk.

As for the book of her life, this is what Sabrina reported:

S: He's opening a book.

A: What does that book look like?

S: It's brown, but the pages are blank. I can't read what's in there. He's telling me to look deeper.

A: So, let's ask Archie how you're supposed to see the information on those blank pages.

S: You have to be willing to see -he said.

A: Are you willing to see?

S: I don't know, I'm a little scared. I'm worried about finding out what's there. In part, I don't want to, but I am also curious.

This is how Sabrina's spirit was encouraged to see the details of her life as a homeless man. Together with her guide, they evaluated the objectives of those experiences and thus she was able to understand the lessons and symptoms that she had brought to her present life as Sabrina.

The Spirit Guides

These are more advanced spirits whose mission is to guide. Their gender depends on what they prefer. There are spirits that consider their energy to be male, some female and others not of a defined gender. It all depends on how they present themselves and the body they have preferred in their previous reincarnations.

Each spirit group has at least one spirit guide assigned to them. Michael Newton describes in his book "Destiny of Souls" that a group can have more than one and even a kind of assistant guide, although the hierarchies there do not exist. A guide has more experience, and it is with this experience that he is willing to guide us when we need or request it. We must remember that human beings have free will, both in the spiritual world and once incarnated.

Our guide helps us to choose the precise lessons for our development, according to the needs we have. He is also the one who helps us to evaluate previous reincarnations. He never leaves us alone, even in the most difficult moments of our lives. If we want his protection and assistance, we only have to ask for it.

Communication with a Guide

To give a better idea of what a guide looks like and what happens when he comes to help us in our transition, I will share a segment from the Luz's session. She had a Life Between Lives session with me. After her death as Marly, Luz started to move away from her physical body as she went up to the spirit world.

Luz: I see a light.

Antonio: Take your time. Move into that light and as you go into it, tell me what you are feeling.

L: Much peace. I just float.

A: Can you describe that light to me?

L: It's a very intense light.

A: Is it just one or do you see others around it?

L: There are others around, but this is the biggest one. In front of it there is a very intense light. I'm going that way.

A: How are those other lights in relation to that big light?

L: Around it.

A: How many lights can you count?

L: There are several small ones, but there is one that is guiding.

A: As you approach that light, tell me if the colors are soft or bright.

L: It's a very intense light.

A: What color is that light?

L: Purple -apparently, it was an advanced spirit.

A: And the lights that are around that purple light, what color are they?

L: White.

A: How does that light receive you? -I asked, referring to the purple light.

L: With much love, but there is a peace that I cannot describe.

A: Does that light produce any other feeling in you?

L: Tranquility. It came to receive me with much love.

A: Does that light have facial characteristics?

L: It doesn't have a body, but it does.

A: How does that supposed body that looks like one but isn't?

L: It is like a triangle that has flashes of light. It's very luminous. Its body is energy.

A: Does that energy transmit information to you?

L: Yes, I am receiving information.

A: Can you repeat the information that is being given to you?

L: I am not yet ready to repeat the information that is being given to me.

Luz's session lasted almost three hours, and when she came out of the hypnotic trance, she didn't remember anything that was said. One of the characteristics of that interview was the blocking of certain information by her guide. It seems that she was still going through tests in her current reincarnation and having access to additional information could be counterproductive to her evolution.

We will continue to analyze the session that Aurelio and I facilitated for Luz in 2016 later, as well as that Life Between Lives session I that I facilitated for her three years later.

Planning for the Next Life (or Reincarnation)

Once the recently completed life is evaluated, it is time to start planning for the next one. This is done on the basis of the lessons we feel we have missed out on, as well as new ones that we will choose for ourselves. Our guide can give us recommendations and suggestions, but it is up to us to make the final decision.

We also choose the geographical place where we will be born, as well as the gender we will have. At this stage, we also make contracts with members of our group or other spiritual groups to play a certain role in our future life.

Let's look at life planning as the elaboration of a play. As in every play, there are main and secondary actors, there are heroes and villains. But at the end of the theater season, it is just a play in which actors play characters. Perhaps, later they will get together to have a cup of coffee and evaluate the artistic success of the show. Those actors are aware that it is merely a role.

In the same way, human beings should remember that this life is a play. We share the stage with other actors who play a role, and together we gain experience and spiritual evolution. There will be characters who will play an absent father, an abusive or self-sacrificing mother. Others will be the unfaithful husband or wife, the son who dies young, the man who abuses them, and so on. Each one of these situations, considered bad in human eyes, brings with it a spiritual lesson. Pain and suffering are amplifiers of learning. It is up to us to choose to learn in love or in suffering.

It is in the planning stage that we also designate the gifts or limitations we will have. In some sessions, I have witnessed clients with a family member who had a birth condition or syndrome seek an explanation for that "punishment" or "grief." To their surprise, once immersed in the spiritual world, we were able to discover that the spirit chose to be born this way to help their family learn about limitless love and non-judgment. That child, who at first sight seemed to have a disadvantage in relation to others, turned out to be an advanced spirit who had offered to reincarnate for the spiritual evolution of that family.

After all these years of facilitating sessions, I have discovered that advanced spirits born with some limitation seek to help their environment evolve more quickly. You only have to look at the members of those families to realize the positivity and love with which they face life. Of course, there will be others who, not understanding that purpose, will deny, lament, and curse that "bad luck," wasting the opportunity to learn what that spirit came to teach them. We can't change the challenges, but we can change our perception, thus avoiding associating a negative energy or emotion to that circumstance.

Reyna and the Body Selection Before Birth

Perhaps I can illustrate this phase of choosing the body with Reyna's session. She came to me for a session using the Michael Newton technique, Live Between Lives.

> **Antonio**: Reyna, as you go to the place where you will select the body you will have in your next reincarnation, please describe to me everything you are seeing.

> **Reyna**: It's an open space with halos of light. I have to go through it.

> **A**: Do you see or feel other beings in this place?

> **R**: No, just John – the guide - and me.

A: During the process of selecting the body, how many choices have you been given?

R: Three.

A: Of those three, how many are male and how many female?

R: All female.

A: Can you test these bodies? -other clients have reported being able to try on bodies in a kind of virtual reality.

R: No, I just have to choose one.

A: Why are you going to choose the body that you will have, Reyna?

R: Because it's going to allow me to focus on things other than appearance.

A: How is that body going to help you not focus on appearance?

R: Because it's a normal body, which has nothing spectacular about it.

A: While you're choosing the body you're going to have, is there anything that John will point out to you in the meantime?

R: He tells me to make sure I choose a body that allows me to focus on things other than myself.

A: Once you've chosen the body, how do you know it's time to reincarnate?

R: Because I feel a force pulling me to do so.

A: Would you say that you reincarnate because you are forced to or because you want to?

R: Because I wish it myself, but at the same time I feel this force that drives me to do it. It is as if it were a kind of motivation.

A: Have you ever resisted reincarnation?

R: Oh, yes.

A: And why was that?

R: Because I thought I wasn't ready.

A: Do you feel ready to reincarnate as Reyna this time?

R: Yes.

Reyna's session lasted three and a half hours. She had gone into such a deep trance that in the end she could hardly answer my questions. When she came out of it, she didn't remember anything.

She had gotten a clear message from this session. She had to focus on anything but herself, since in a past life she had stayed in her comfort zone, which delayed the beginning of her mission in that life. This time she was making sure to remove any distractions from the path to complete her pending goals.

Contracts

Contracts are agreements among spirits of the same or different group to interact during their reincarnation. In the same way, spirits have the freedom to choose when and where to be born, which directly influences the tests they will have to go through. We can also make contracts with other spirits of our own free will. With them, we will be able to interact in different scenarios, helping us to evolve.

It is during the establishment of the contracts that we also choose who will be our points of support in life, our guides and those who will make us go through difficult and painful situations as well. Let's remember that, in the spiritual world, there is neither good nor bad. There is no judgement, and we are guided with love. Unfortunately, many times we are our own worst judges and executioners, when in reality no one pressures us to be perfect.

Robert Schwartz, a former American marketing consultant who, after having a session with a medium, decided to investigate the spiritual world and write about it, has published extensive information about the pre-birth planning stage. In his book "Your Soul's Plan," he explains in detail the pre-birth planning of different people who experienced tragic situations, such as the death of a child, a terrorist attack, alcoholism, being the father of a drug addict, or having contracted the AIDS virus.

The author explains in detail, the planning of each event they would experience and the people they would interact with. He even shows that accidents are not really accidents, but situations that we previously planned so that they would cause a change in the direction of our lives, or so that we could awaken spiritually.

Through sessions with my clients, I have been able to confirm this. Some experience the heartbreak, abandonment, or deception of parents and couples, while others may experience the pain of losing a child at an early age, being orphaned as a child, or being given up for adoption. All of this has a purpose.

So, if we ourselves are agreeing with other spirits to play the role of victimizers in our lives, does that make us victims? If we arranged those painful interactions, does that mean that those spirits are evil?

No and no. It is up to us to determine the meaning we give to an event. If we allow a negative emotion to be associated with an event that caused us pain, we will be creating what we know as a trauma. This will remain engraved in our subconscious, affecting us throughout our lives. Since the soul does not understand the past, present, and future, it can become trapped in that experience causing different physical or psychological manifestations in the future. Our soul may be in the now, but also tied to that experience of the past.

Therefore, it is key to remember that what we have lived is the result of agreements we ourselves made with other spirits, which have a hidden lesson. We just need to ask ourselves what our spirit thought it should learn when it planned this lesson before being born.

We should not run away from difficult experiences. Instead, let's embrace them and let our spirit experience everything it needs from it. If we are feeling pain, then let's feel it. If we lose a loved one, let our soul learn what loss and emptiness feel like. After all, we have reincarnated to do something we cannot do as spirits: learn and evolve through emotions.

Karma

Karma is a concept of the Hindu religion, which starts from the principle of cause and effect, where the actions of an individual (cause) influence the future of himself (effect).

Many have a misconception about it. They see karma as a punishment for something that was done or said, as an acquired debt that we must pay. Karma, on a spiritual level, is the law of balance. For example, if in this life one takes someone's life, it is more likely that in another life one must give life to that spirit. If we made someone feel something at a certain moment, it is most likely that later we will experience the same thing with equal or greater intensity.

I have had several sessions in which the client told me that he had always had a bad relationship with one of his parents. The person could not find any justification for this feeling. He simply couldn't stand them. During the session, looking for the origin of that emotion, he went to a past life where his parent in this life was an enemy who ended up killing him. This time, they had come together to work on their relationship and to learn to forgive from love. Like this case, I have had several that perfectly illustrate the concept of karma.

I still remember the day my wife, Catherine, asked me to facilitate a hypnosis session with Giselle, a friend of hers from school. I had known her for a long time too; Catherine introduced me to Giselle at the age of eighteen.

By that time, Giselle had already gone through some pretty sad circumstances with her mother. One of them was the death of her

father during her childhood, causing her a strong feeling of abandonment and of being incomplete. As her life developed, her poor
relationship with her mother continued to cause problems that were
reflected in their relationship.

When I started the session with Giselle, she went into a deep
trance very quickly. While we were looking for the source of the
symptoms she had, she went to a past life where she was a tall, strong
farmer named Miguel. He described the place and his clothing in
great detail: jeans, shoes and a straw hat.

Despite having a difficult job, that man's life was absolutely happy. He had a wife and daughters. When he told me about his life, his
farm and his family, Giselle's face lit up with joy. The farmer even told
me about the birth of his grandson, unable to hold back his tears as
he held him in his arms for the first time.

That happy life was definitely a contrast to the one he now was
living as Giselle. As time went on, we found out that this man fell
into bed because of a long illness, which consumed him little by little. When he was weak and close to his death, I asked him if there
was anyone looking after him. His answer was: "my daughter Ariana."
I asked him to look into her eyes, explaining that the eyes are the
windows to the soul. I asked him if those eyes were or would be in
Giselle's life. His response, in a voice of surprise, was: it's my mom!
Ariana was now Giselle's mother.

During her life as a farmer, Giselle had experienced what it was
like to be happy, to be cared for and looked after with love and care
while he could not look after himself. What is interesting is that, in
her current life, it was now her turn to take care of her mother, who
had been lying in bed for a few years due to a brain condition. Now it
was her turn to assist the spirit that had cared for her in her past life.
It was simply the law of balance.

If we were to understand this universal principle, we would not
have to regret the situations we have experienced, nor judge certain

people badly. Perhaps the term for a human being who causes us suffering should be ignorant. For example, if a rapist were aware of the existence of the law of karma, he would not dare to rape a woman. If he knew that it is absolutely certain that he will have to experience a rape with the same or greater intensity in a future reincarnation, perhaps he would not do so.

The truth is that our past has defined our present, and our present will be what defines our future. By this, I mean not only in this life, but beyond. Linear time is a creation of the human brain in order to understand time, but in the spirit world it does not exist. There is only the "now." We may have been reincarnated in Egypt three thousand years ago, but for our spirit, that just happened. While we use the term lives, for the spirit that never dies, there is only one life with experiences in different bodies. That's why everything we've done or been told in other lives is latent in the current reincarnation with its consequences.

Our free will and actions affect, from now on, what we will experience in the future. As we make decisions and exercise our freedom along with the cause and effect of all our actions, it is as if we are creating alternative time lines in the future. Death is only an illusion. What dies is the body, but the spirit is eternal and will carry within its reincarnation any learning, symptom or traumatic event that was not processed correctly.

The Spirit World

The spirit world is perceived as our true home, because our natural form is that of spirit. The body is only a suit that we temporarily inhabit in order to be able to function in this earthly school.

Throughout the sessions I have conducted, my clients have described this space as a city with buildings with different purposes. We cannot prove if everything they say during the trance is totally correct though. They may be giving us a description based on what their senses and mind know about this planet, this reality. But what is really striking is that people of different ages, cultures, religious beliefs, nationalities, and languages report basically the same thing.

Other clients see a transparent city, as if it were made of glass. Some report that the spirits that inhabit it are flesh and blood people wearing white robes, while others describe them as bodies of energy or light. Chico Xavier's book, "Nosso Lar," and the film based on it, give an excellent graphic description of what this place looks like.

The Indigenous and the Spiritual World

I decided to return to Gina's session, as it is very rich in spiritual information. She belongs to the 3% of people who do not remember anything that happened while they were in a hypnotic trance.

At the end of the Introspective Hypnosis course I taught in Peru at the beginning of 2017, I decided to do a demonstration session with one of the students attending the course. Gina, a 24-year-old woman, had contacted me from the city of Cusco to express her interest in attending my class. Thus, with enthusiasm and determination, she traveled to the city of Lima.

I have a habit of making my students experience what it feels like to be in a trance before I proceed to teach them and demonstrate how hypnotic inductions work. I think that once a person learns the steps to reach this state, it is more difficult for them to enter into a hypnotic trance.

During the induction exercises, I noticed that Gina would go into a deep trance very quickly, even just by doing the suggestibility tests. That is why, at the end of the course, I decided to choose her to do a demonstration.

As expected, she entered quickly into a deep trance. We started by working on sad memories of this life, and then I asked her subconscious to show her a past reincarnation that was relevant to the situations she was facing in the present one.

Gina went to a life where she was an indigenous woman, who was happy with her husband and son, and without major problems. One of the crucial moments of that existence was when her children, now grown up, were ready to leave home. She felt sad because, I think, deep down she knew she would never see them again. As we neared the end of that life, she was lying in bed.

Antonio: I want you to go to the last minute of that life. Tell me what is happening.

Indigenous Woman: I am coughing a lot.

A: How does your body feel?

IW: Weak.

A: Are you very old?

IW: No.

A: Is anyone there with you?

IW: My husband.

A: Where are you?

IW: In my house, in my bed. I want to leave now, -She answered in a very soft voice.

I continued to ask questions to find out what symptoms she had had during that death to determine if she had brought them into his current body. To do this, I asked her to go to the moment she was leaving the physical body.

A: Are you out yet?

IW: Yes.

A: What do you see down there?

IW: Clouds. I am floating.

A: Do you feel that you are going up?

IW: Yes, I feel light.

A: If you analyzed that life, what do you think you had to learn?

IW: Not to settle for living there all my life. I would have liked to know other places.

Gina, in her current life, faced the same challenge. It was common for her to get stuck whenever she started something new. She was also insecure, so her spirit was telling me that she had not passed that test. In this life, she would have to face the same challenge, because everything that we did not complete in a previous life, we bring to a next one. Since in the spirit world there is only the "now," I asked Gina's spirit to give her advice for this life, to give her a better understanding of the actions she should correct.

I know the concept is a little difficult to understand, but basically, I was communicating with her Higher Self, the part that is connected to the spirit world. That part knows what is pending and where we should focus in this reincarnation. If we look at it from a practical point of view, it was like asking Gina to give advice to herself.

Antonio: What advice would you give Gina for this life?

Higher Self: To travel. She is afraid to leave her familiar home.

A: Is she afraid to make the same mistake?

HS: Yes.

A: Then what do we tell her?

HS: To explore.

A: Gina told me that every time she wants to undertake something, she blocks herself. Is that because of the way you lived?

HS: It's the fear she has.

A: Can you help me remove that fear?

HS: Yes.

A: Great! Because we see what happens when she lets herself be dominated by fear and stays in one place.

HS: Yes. There is nothing to lose.

We continued the session by removing those fears with the help of the spirit of the indigenous woman. In the meantime, I continued to probe the points she wanted to work on in the session, as well as more advice for her.

When I felt that we already knew everything we needed to know, I asked her to go ahead and tell me what she saw.

G: I see a lot of light.

A: Go into the light, which is the source from which we all come. Tell me what you feel when you enter it.

G: I feel happy -she answered as her face suddenly lit up.

A: Move to the moment you reach your destination, and tell me if you see others like you.

G: It's a garden! I see people in white.

A: Do you recognize this garden? Is it a familiar place to you?

G: We come here to rest and then we study.

A: What do you study?

G: Some white and gold books.

A: What is in those books?

G: Lessons.

A: Lessons about what?

G: About us, about what we must learn.

I already knew this information from the books I had studied when I started learning hypnosis. What Gina was describing was only a confirmation of what I already knew and what other clients had manifested to me while in a trance.

One of the first things the American hypnotherapist, Dolores Cannon, taught me when I took her Quantum Healing Hypnosis Technique course, was not to ask questions that would lead the person to answer things that the hypnotherapist is assuming. It is key to ask questions as if you don't know about the subject, because we must not limit their experience, nor assume what the client is perceiving.

A: Who studies with you?

G: Souls.

A: Do you have someone to direct you or do you study what you want?

G: Here we come to rest -she replied, as if to say that this was not the place to ask questions.

I asked the spirit to go ahead to the time when he was leaving the rest area.

A: Where are you going after the resting place?

G: With my companions.

A: And how many are there in your group?

G: Seven.

A: Are some of your companions in your current life as Gina?

G: Yes.

A: Can you tell me who they are?

G: My mom and my brothers.

A: What is your name in that place, in the spirit world?

G: Andrean -she answered with surprise and some difficulty in pronouncing it. Something like that.

A: Look at your energy and tell me what color it is.

G: Blue with gold.

A: And the color of the energy of the others in your group?

G: The same.

A: Do you have someone to guide or lead you? How does that work?

G: We have guides, but they are like a support. We ask them things we want to know.

A: Do they tell you what to do?

G: No, we decide.

A: So, it's not like a chain of command where you report to each other?

G: No.

A: Go to the moment when you plan your reincarnation as Gina and tell me the lesson you are choosing.

G: What happens is that the body is dense -she smiled, referring to the third dimension in which we live. It's difficult-. Life is difficult.

A: On Earth?

G: Yes.

A: Why have you chosen to live as Gina? What is your purpose?

G: To trust her wisdom, no matter how difficult life is.

The session continued, while I took the time to ask all the necessary questions. It is not advisable to keep a person in a trance for too long, especially someone like Gina who was in a very deep trance.

Gina's spirit began to talk about her mission, about her mother in this life and how to help her with the confusion she was in. Gina's mother had her own business and was completely focused on it. The message was not to forget the purpose she had in this life, to learn, like Gina, about hypnosis. Together they would help others, just as I had done.

By the year 2020, about three years after that session, Gina's mother had learned Aurelio Mejia's method and Dolores Cannon's Quantum Healing Hypnosis Technique. Now, both of them facilitate sessions and give workshops in different cities of Peru. What Gina's spirit and her guide had said had become true. Learning hypnosis was part of her learning.

Back in the session, I asked her if it was possible for us to contact her guide.

A: What do you call your guides when you need them?

G: We call their energy.

A: Could we call him to answer some of our questions?

G: He can't

This is not unusual. Some guides are very communicative and willing to help us by clarifying our doubts, but there are others who are stricter and prefer not to answer. The guides are practical and direct. Not being ruled by emotions, they do not hesitate to give us a good ear-pull when necessary.

Since Gina was pregnant during the session, I took the opportunity to ask her spirit a few more questions.

A: Is it possible to know who in your group is going to be Gina's child?

This information had been obtained during the induction exercises a couple of days ago, when we communicated with the spirit of the one who would be her next child.

G: Yes, it's my partner.

A: Have you been together before?

G: Yes, he wanted to come -she answered with a big smile.

A: Ask your companion what he wants to tell you before he is born as your son.

G: That that was what had to happen, that he had to come. He's part of the group.

A: Is there anything he wants to tell you?

G: Yes, that we have the same energy.

Gina's session lasted two hours, during which we were able to work on several issues, such as programming her body to be anesthetized at the time of delivery so she would not feel pain. Since her spirit was in the spirit world, we asked her for advice for each of the course participants. Everyone was amazed when Gina's spirit mentioned the problems each one was going through, and then advised them about them. We should keep in mind that Gina had come from Cusco and did not know any of the other participants, nor had she interacted with them before the course.

When I took her out of the hypnotic trance, Gina thought that half an hour had passed and she didn't remember anything that had happened. While I was talking to the other participants, analyzing what had taken place in their session, she was just looking at us strangely.

Although it is normal to remember everything that happened during the trance, for many, not remembering is validating that what was experienced was real and not imagined.

THE STUDY OF HYPNOSIS

After my mother-in-law's death in 2012, Catherine brought with her a few books that she found among her things. One of them was, "Many Lives Many Masters," by American doctor and psychiatrist Brian Weiss. In that book, the author relates how he discovered past lives through hypnosis, while treating a patient he named Catherine. After it came into my hands, I read it in one day. I quickly realized that I had found what I had been looking for. I had always had the desire to help. I was always looking for something that I could not define or explain, until that book came to me. In this wonderful episode of my life and everything that followed, I will go deeper later, by telling you about my teachers and the points that conspired in my path to devote myself to regressive hypnosis. This will only be a brief introduction.

Although by that time, I had begun to learn to read the Egyptian tarot, I abandoned this tool because I felt it was not for me. In 2013, and after evaluating it with Catherine, I made the decision to learn hypnosis. The first classes I took were with Dolores Cannon, who listed her training courses in Quantum Healing Hypnosis Technique (QHHT) on her website. It was with this technique that I had my first experiences taking my clients into past lives in search of answers and a better understanding of who they are and what their purpose is for in this life.

As I practiced Dolores' method, I also gained more experience and, at the same time, the clients who came to me presented more complex cases. It was as if the universe or my guides, knew I was ready for them. In fact, this pattern continues to repeat itself to this day. As I learn new techniques, the opportunity and, above all, the need to use them appears in my next sessions. I simply have no choice.

As time went on, I noticed that my sessions were manifesting situations that required techniques that Quantum Hypnosis Healing Technique did not provide, such as assisting lost spirits attached to my clients' energy field.

By the year 2015, I contacted the assistant of the hypnotherapist Aurelio Mejía, whom I had been following for over a year. As fate would have it, my wife and I offered our home in North Carolina as a meeting place for him and his clients and he gladly accepted. That is how we were able to host him in our home, and have the opportunity to learn his Introspective Hypnosis technique, while I witnessed and participated in the thirty-eight sessions he had.

The teaching I received from seeing Aurelio in action was invaluable. His innate ability to connect with people, to accompany them on a journey through their traumatic memories, and thus change their perception through forgiveness therapy and help them withdraw the negative emotion associated with that event, was impressive. At all times, he took it upon himself to break down any myths about hypnosis by showing me and my colleague and friend, Genoveva Calleja, in a simple way, how to get to the root cause of the symptom the person was presenting.

In the year 2016, I had the opportunity to receive him at my home again, where I refined his technique further, solving the doubts that had arisen while practicing on my own. One of the things that I noticed as soon as I learned the tools that Aurelio used, was that the type of client that came to me had changed. People were no longer coming in search of a spiritual awakening, but rather people with psychosomatic symptoms, such as phobias, fears, depression, addictions, and sadness.

Little by little, I identified myself more with that technique and with the new role I had been given, while I accompanied my clients in their self-healing process. At the same time, my style and approach during the session were transformed as I saw that most of my clients had gone through traumatic incidents in childhood and adolescence. These events had caused them fear and insecurity, and had diminished their self-esteem, which resulted in them falling into a victim role and pattern that affected every aspect of their lives.

Some others had been physically or emotionally abused, either within the family or within the marriage, which eventually had the same effect: adopting the role of victim, having low self-esteem, and not feeling worthy of being happy.

Through forgiveness therapy, commonly used by Aurelio, I saw how they freed themselves from those emotions and understood the purpose of that experience. Every traumatic event has a lesson. Remember María's session, which I mentioned in the first part of this book. She was abandoned by her mother at the age of five, which triggered various traumas and sadness. During the session we had, we discovered that those events had a purpose. Her spirit had planned that experience before she was born in order to learn to be independent and to learn to love each other.

After learning Aurelio's Introspective Hypnosis technique, lost spirits also began to manifest themselves attached to my clients' energy field, causing them various symptoms. As the Argentinean hypnotherapist, José Luis Cabouli, says in his book, "Terapia de la Posesión Espiritual," a regression therapist, sooner or later, will encounter spirits in his sessions, whether he likes it or not.

The Patient Grandmother

Among the spirits that began to manifest themselves in the sessions I conducted were also the deceased loved ones who came to communicate with their family members or who were simply lost and had not gone into the light. On more than one occasion, I was told that they had been waiting for the opportunity to communicate with my client, either to tell them they were fine or to give them a specific message.

To understand how this can happen, I will share the dialogue that took place during the Victoria session in February, 2019. Victoria felt great sorrow over the death of a good friend of hers a few years ago. Since she had a negative emotion associated with that event, before starting the session, I decided to give John - her friend - the opportunity to communicate and help her with her process.

As I always tell my students, anyone in an altered or expanded state of consciousness is a potential medium. That's how communication was established between them. John's spirit spoke to Victoria about the forgiveness process. He told her that she should forgive him for leaving, that he had already fulfilled his lessons to learn in this life, and that he was ready to leave. He also asked her to forgive him for promising that he would always be by her side. Victoria forgave him, while I explained to her that, in reality, John was always present, and that now she had to learn to feel differently.

Victoria has the gift of clairvoyance and seeing spirits; however, she had a hard time accepting it and understanding why she had it. John made it clear to her that, for her, having this gift meant freedom because it helped her to fulfill her mission. One of the problems she had brought to the meeting was her nervousness about seeing spirits, believing that some of those energies could be negative. John took it upon himself to explain to her that negative energies don't exist, and told her that he was working on teaching and showing her things through her son - Victoria's son -. He continued the conversation by saying that she doubted herself because she didn't know if the thoughts she had were hers or from other spirits.

At the time of the session, Victoria was in severe physical pain. I knew there was an energy, a spirit, that was trying to communicate, but I asked her to wait a moment while we worked on other symptoms, and to please ease her pain in the meantime. When I asked John if there were other spirits near us, he said yes, there were many.

Antonio: John, before starting the session, Victoria had felt a very strong physical pain. Whose pain is it?

John: Someone else's.

A: Are there others here?

J: Yes, -she answered, shaking her head and smiling-. There are many.

A: I promised this person that we would help her.

J: It's a woman -said John without letting me finish.

A: I promised that woman that if she would stop feeling that pain, we would help her. What do you say we help her, John?

J: That's it.

A: What's the best way? Can I talk to her through Victoria?

J: No - she answered by shaking her head from side to side.

A: How do we do that?

J: She wants to talk.

A: Who wants to talk?

J: Her grandmother.

A: Is it her grandmother? And why the physical pain then?

J: In the world - she meant when she had a body - she had diabetes. She suffered a lot.

A: Is she grandma Blanca?

J: Yes.

A: Well, let's welcome her - Victoria's face began to fill with joy.

A: Grandma, you can use your granddaughter's body and communicate.

Blanca: Finally! Finally! -said Grandma smiling and crying with emotion-. Thank you!

A: What do you think, Grandma?

B: Thank you!

A: No, thank you for the communication.

B: Finally!

A: What do we say to your granddaughter?

B: I've waited so long!

A: Grandma, why did you wait so long?

B: Because I knew she was special.

A: And the wait was because she was afraid?

B: Yes, she wasn't ready.

A: She wasn't, past tense. Let's see, Grandma, take away that fear and doubt. Give her courage. Tell her what you want to tell her, we hear you.

B: You are so special, Victoria. Don't be afraid. Nothing is going to hurt you. Many are waiting for you, many. Your children need to see who you really are.

Thus, communication with Victoria's grandmother continued. She told her how important it was to accept this gift and work with her children, since one of them could feel more than the rest, and the other had visions of the future. The three of them were a team. She explained that she should not be afraid because she had not been sent alone to this reincarnation. There were more by her side.

Victoria's session was very beautiful and emotional. It had to take place because there was a message that John's and Grandma Blanca's spirits had to give her about her gift, her children's gifts, and forgiveness.

Victoria was just one of several people with special gifts that have been sent to my office. They came to a session because there was a message they needed to receive, because they needed to understand that the gift they possessed had to be used to help others.

In Victoria's case, being able to see spirits could help them go into the light. Her grandmother, Blanca, had waited patiently for the opportunity to speak with her. She had certainly tried to communicate with Victoria many times before, but perhaps Victoria's fear and nervousness had made it impossible for her to recognize her grandmother.

Many of the people with these kinds of abilities who came to my office wanted nothing to do with their gift, and some even wished they didn't have it. I can imagine how difficult it must be for a child to see spirits, or feel them at night in their room, without understanding what is happening. But it must be even more difficult for those little ones to grow up with parents who don't know about metaphysics, who treat them as if they were hallucinating, who take them to psychologists or priests, or who simply ignore them.

This is how I developed my practice over the next few years, with experiences, messages, and self-healing, while guiding my clients to heal themselves. Over time, I learned the technique, Life Between Lives, from Michael Newton, and TVP (Past Life Therapy) from

José Luis Cabouli, which gave me the tools I needed to develop my own style.

2019 was a fabulous year. Finally, after introspection combined with the messages transmitted by mediums and my client's spirit guides, I resigned my job to dedicate myself fully to regressive hypnosis, which continues to become better known as a healing therapy. I will talk about this in detail later in the chapter, Signs and Messages.

That year was one of much growth, where the universe opened the doors to all that I had been holding back. I taught eight courses online with the assistance of my colleague Alba Weinman and my wife Catherine; three courses in the United States, one in New Zealand, and another in Holland. From then on, I felt that everything I was doing finally made sense. Even the courses I have taught and the sessions I have facilitated during the Covid-19 pandemic in 2020, have developed favorably. Nothing has been able to stop the path drawn by each person and their spiritual evolution.

What Is Hypnosis?

On the Internet, there is a lot of information about it, so what I will do is explain hypnosis from my point of view and therapeutic approach. By this I do not mean that my technique is the only one or that it is the best, as there are many that can achieve the same result. My intention is to show how I use it.

Hypnosis is an altered state of consciousness, which means that the person is conscious at all times. With it, what we do is focus all attention on something specific - on our instructions, in this case - to get beyond the critical mind and access the subconscious.

In other words, we hypnotherapists try to set aside the conscious mind while working with the subconscious, which is where all our memories and associations, both negative and positive, are stored.

What Is the Conscious Mind?

It is the part of the mind where reason, logic, and analytical skills are located. According to studies in psychology, the conscious area constitutes 12% of our mind. From a spiritual point of view, its function is to ensure the survival of the physical body. When we face a traumatic situation that overloads us and/or makes it difficult for us to process it, the conscious mind encapsulates it and sends it to the subconscious mind, where it will be kept until we are ready to deal with that repressed emotion.

For this reason, it is not uncommon to hear from clients who do not remember some or much of their childhood. To me, it is just an indication that there may be traumatic events during childhood that will need to be worked through.

What Is the Critical Mind?

The critical mind is what divides the conscious from the subconscious, a kind of guardian that watches over what enters and what does not enter our subconscious. We can imagine it as the password to enter a computer before being able to access it, to obtain or save information.

Why did most of our traumas or repressed emotions originate during our childhood? The answer is simple. During our childhood, the critical mind is not fully developed and that is why every traumatic event goes straight to the subconscious. These are situations that tomorrow, when we are adults, will make us react just as we would have reacted at the age that was created in our subconscious, without knowing why.

What Is the Subconscious Mind?

It is the repository of our memories and associations to internal maps and our repressed emotions. For example, in the subconscious of a smoker, perhaps there is the association that a cigarette is equivalent to relaxation; for a drug addict, the drug may be equivalent to not feeling.

For the subconscious, time does not exist and everything happens in the now. I could have had an incident with a dog that wanted to bite me when I was four years old, but for my subconscious that just happened, and every time I see a dog, no matter how old I am, I will react the same way I did when I was four years old.

From my point of view, information is recorded in the subconscious in three ways: through trauma, through repetition, and through visualization. The subconscious works like a kind of digital video recorder, recording everything that has happened to us in this and other lives. Accessing the information stored in the subconscious, while my clients are in a trance, is how I can look for the origin of this or that symptom that afflicts them now.

Fear of Worms

To better explain the function of the subconscious and how it can be accessed during a hypnosis session, I will refer again to María's session, about which I wrote at the beginning of this book.

Near the end of María's session, and while reading the notes from my interview with her, I decided it was time to look for the root cause of her fear of worms. She had told me about her fear of them, but when I asked her if she had had any incidents with them, she said she didn't remember any.

María's session had been very intense up until that point. We visited several traumatic events in her life, most of which were related to her mother. Her mother had caused her and her brother a lot of pain in revenge for their father's abandonment.

Antonio: María, I want you to place yourself at the origin of your fear of worms, in this life or another. You are spirit and there are no limits.

María: There are many worms! -she said, shaking her head from side to side, with an expression of disgust on her face.

A: Where are you?

M: In a garden -she answered with a quick breath.

A: How old are you there?

M: Two years old.

A: And in that place, is your name María too? -I asked her, trying to understand if it was a memory of this or another life.

M: María.

A: And are you playing in that garden?

M: No! -she answered almost shouting, My mother! It's my mother! -she said, bursting into tears.

A: Look at it from outside. That's over now and it's not going to affect you.

M: She wants me to eat them!

María's mother had done many horrible things in revenge for her father. This event was the last of several similar ones we worked on during her session. I continued for a few more minutes, navigating through that memory until the moment when she was able to transform that fear and forgive her mother. The session had been very intense and María was completely exhausted.

Her case is a clear example of how all our memories are stored in the subconscious. The event with the worms was one that was not consciously accessible, but it was there, as if time had not passed, causing her terrible fear every time she saw worms, even from afar.

It has never ceased to amaze me that, in one session, a person would go into a memory of the early years of his life and describe the event in great detail, when in fact they did not even remember it consciously. There are even times when, in search of the origin of a symptom, my clients have gone back to the time when they were in their mother's womb, recounting the thoughts, feelings and experiences of their parents during the months of pregnancy.

REGRESSIVE HYPNOSIS

This is a type of hypnosis that consists of taking a person, who is in an altered state of consciousness, back in time to relive events from the past, while being guided by the therapist, whose function is to facilitate a better understanding of those events in order to help change that erroneous perception, which caused a negative emotion to be associated with it, thus triggering different symptoms in the present.

The symptom is the thread that will lead us to another experience, which may be in a past life, intrauterine life, early childhood, or perhaps a little later. This physical or psychological manifestation is usually associated with the agony of the body in a past life.

But why do we speak of a bad perception lodged in our subconscious? The explanation lies in the fact that the events and associations that were recorded in our subconscious did so in a distorted way. All external events first pass through a series of filters, such as our memories, beliefs, basic needs, meta programs -a kind of template we use to solve problems, always in the same way- values and past decisions.

Once that event passes the filters, it creates an association, like an internal map that can also be affected by our state of mind.

It is based on these internal maps that we relate to the world, as explained by doctor and psychologist Milton Erickson. In addition, they are also what make us react within a certain context. From this point of view, one could say that there is no right or wrong behavior, since we are only reacting within that context.

When the individual, assisted by the therapist, understands what really happened and understands that, from all those events we learn and evolve, the negative emotion is replaced by a positive one. This automatically makes the symptom that it caused, disappear.

Regression to Past Lives and the Illusion of Time

The same concept explained above also applies to past lives. Traumatic events, such as the tragic death of the body, incidents not properly processed by our spirit, patterns of behavior and relationships with other people, manifest physically, such as pain, fears, phobias, resentment, illness, and disease. These symptoms end up constantly affecting life today.

This can be better understood thanks to the concept of non-time, which holds that the past, present, and future do not exist, since everything is happening in the now. This is exemplified in the Introspective Hypnosis technique that I practice and teach, which, unlike others, focuses on the spirit and not the mind. While the mind is limited to what is happening in this dimension, the spirit, which never dies and is multidimensional, provides me with all the information I need in a session.

Going back to the previous explanation, we must understand that spirit does not understand time. One may have lived previously in the Inca Empire, in the 1400s, but for our spirit, that just took place. If some traumatic event of that reincarnation was not processed correctly, or if the spirit did not process the death of the body correctly, we will see the repercussions in the current life. For example, if in that past life we died by drowning in a river, in this life you will most likely be afraid of lakes or the sea because, for our spirit, death by drowning is still happening in another timeline.

If everything is happening now, why do we use the term past life? Actually, we do it to have a better understanding of what we are going through, to give a more earthly and human meaning to reincarnations. But the truth is that they are all happening now in another timeline. That's why, as everything happens now, and for the spirit it's one life with experiences in different bodies, all that we are experiencing in those simultaneous or parallel lives are affecting us here and now in the current life. Dr. José Luis Cabouli explains this concept in his book, "Atrapamiento y Recuperación del Alma" (Entrapment and Recovery of the Soul), which I have been able to confirm and recreate with my clients.

When an event in a past reincarnation was not processed correctly, our energy is trapped in time in that event, causing a symptom in our current body. It is the same thing that happens when a trauma is recorded in the subconscious, making us react the same way and age we did when that memory occurred.

Based on the fact that our spirit has lived in many other bodies before, and that in some of those lives, it was forced to experience traumatic situations that were not processed correctly, using the concept of multi-simultaneity, we can then understand that many of the symptoms we present today may have come from other lives that are taking place now, in another timeline.

Without trying to confuse the reader, I would like to pose the following question: if time does not exist and everything happens now, if our spirit is living in other parallel lives, if it is in the current body that we are experiencing certain physical symptoms, should we travel in time and space to another life in search of their origin in order to work on them?

It is at this point that some therapists' approaches and beliefs differ. If the symptom is felt now and is being provoked by something that is happening on a subconscious level in another life, we would not have to travel in time and space to look for it. According to my perspective and the concepts that I have been able to confirm and recreate in my own sessions, we should focus on making conscious what is unconscious or subconscious for us at this time. It is a matter of focusing on the now.

The symptom is the thread that will lead us to another reincarnation. This physical manifestation will surely be linked to the way that body died, in its agony.

One of the most difficult concepts to believe and understand in hypnosis is the concept of time and space. As I mentioned earlier, the spirit or soul does not understand time. It does not know what the past, present, or future is, because for it, only the now exists. The memories that one travels to during a hypnosis session, by being in an altered or expanded state of consciousness, are happening now.

While it is true that, from the point of view of our third dimensional world, the event took place in the past, for the person in the trance, it is taking place now. It is under that premise that we navigate that memory or event. Many will wonder why force a person to relive a traumatic or sad memory? If the incident has already taken place, how does it benefit us to visit again? Wouldn't it aggravate the situation?

When working with trauma, the right way to desensitize it is to allow the person to experience it again to some degree, but this time accompanied by the therapist, who will guide them through different questions. The idea is to help the person change their perception of what actually happened, which will allow the negative emotion associated with that memory to change, allowing the symptom to disappear.

In addition, the client will be reminded of who they are and what they came for, understand the hidden lesson behind that traumatic or sad event, and understand that there are no victims in this school called planet Earth. It was our own spirit that planned those lessons before we were reincarnated. I will go deeper into this concept later.

The Man in the Wheelchair

To better explain this concept, I would like to review Elvira's session. In November, 2019, during the Introspective Hypnosis course I was teaching with the help of Alba, Elvira, Petri, and a small group of class attendees, we gathered in one of the hotel rooms in order to help Elvira relieve a pain she was feeling in her hand.

Petri, a practitioner and teacher of various energy healing modalities who had attended the course from Finland, offered to help. Someone asked me if I would like to witness what they were doing and I accepted, as I was very interested.

When I entered the room, Elvira was sitting in a chair while Petri finished the energy procedure in front of a few more sitting around her. I only saw the last two minutes, but immediately I noticed that Elvira's face was flushed, as if she was hot, and she had started to feel very emotional. Petri explained to her that this was normal when the blockages that did not allow her energy to flow freely, were removed. As Petri, the others, and I talked about why he had decided to learn hypnosis as a complement to her healing practice, I noticed out of the corner of my eye that Elvira was getting even more emotional; so much so that within minutes her tears turned to a flood and her body began to shake.

Petri had definitely managed to unlock something in her, and the repressed emotions were surfacing in front of us. When Petri approached Elvira to try something else, I asked him permission to assist her at that moment. He generously agreed. I sat next to Elvira, as she continued to cry and shake. The symptom was there and she was already in an altered state of consciousness, in a kind of hypnotic trance.

Antonio: Elvira, I want you to take a breath and close your eyes. Focus on that emotion you are experiencing. Where in your body are you feeling it?

Elvira: In the heart.

A: If you could know, if you could imagine, what does that pain feel like?

E: Like a stab.

A: I want you to focus on that sting, on that pain. I'm going to count from one to three and with each number we're going to intensify that condition. Allow your body to do whatever it has to do to feel it. One. Feel the pain more intensely. Two. Even more intense. Three. Much more intense.

As the pain intensified, I could see how her body was experiencing it. Elvira continued crying and shaking.

A: Now, I am going to count from three to one and you will go to the first moment in which you felt this pain. Three, two, one. You are already there. Where do you think you are?

E: It's dark -she said crying-. I feel tight and I can't move my legs. I can't take it anymore with this limitation. I feel paralyzed! I can't do this anymore!

A: Look and pay attention. Where do you think you are?

E: In my mother's womb -she said after a few moments, as she moved her body into a fetal position with her legs and arms shrunken.

A: See if you can hear your mother's heartbeat.

E: Yes.

A: Tell me if you can feel your mother's emotions.

E: Yes, she is anxious and worried.

A: Tell me what you are feeling or thinking while you are in your mother's womb.

E: I feel tight, I can't move my legs. I am afraid and I don't want to be born. This is very difficult, why do I have to do it again?

A: Feeling tight, not being able to move your legs, being afraid to be born, how does it affect your life?

E: It makes me confused and unable to make decisions.

A: And this confusion and not being able to make decisions, what does it keep you from doing in your life?

E: Moving forward, I feel that I can't move forward.

A: Now I want you to move to the moment you are going to be born. One, two, three.

E: I feel tight and I can't move. I begin to see a light, but I don't want to be born. Now there's a very intense light and I'm very cold -she said, shivering with cold.

Elvira had gone from being hot and flushed to feeling very cold. She was born in Russia and after the session she could confirm with her mother that the day she was born the temperature was very low.

A: Now, I want you to pay attention to everything that is happening around you.

E: I don't hear anyone anymore. I seem to have been left alone -she said, breaking into tears-. I don't understand why I am alone.

A: Do you feel your mother near you?

E: No, she's not there and I'm afraid.

A: And how does feeling cold, fear, and loneliness affect you in your life?

E: It makes me dependent.

A: And what does this stop you from doing?

E: It keeps me from moving forward.

Elvira's spirit was trapped in that time, in her birth. Although it is true that it happened when she was a newborn, that event (trauma) was affecting her in her day by day.

Elvira had pronounced a key phrase that made me suspect that what she felt in her mother's womb before she was born was linked to another event from a past life. She said that she could no longer deal with that limitation, that she felt paralyzed and could no longer do it. It was a matter of finding out where those words were coming from, of making conscious what was previously unconscious for her.

A: Elvira, now I am going to count from three to one and I want you to allow your spirit to go to the next event that you think you have to work on today. Let your body do everything it needs to do to relive that experience. Three, two, one. You are already there.

E: I am a man and I am in a wheelchair.

A: Tell me how you feel there.

E: Limited. I can't move, it's not easy.

Elvira had found a past reincarnation related to the symptom she was feeling in the current body. In the life of the man in the wheelchair, he was experiencing a limitation, that of not being able to move his legs and therefore not feeling able to move forward.

We continued to navigate in that past life until the moment of the death of that body. It is always important to take the person through the death of the body to understand what other symptoms he may have brought from that life.

A: Now, I want you to go to the last moment of that life and tell me what is happening.

E: I am older. I am in a hospital and I feel weak. My body feels numb.

A: Who is with you?

E: No one.

A: Now, move to the moment you leave the body and tell me what you see and feel.

E: I see my body below. I feel free at last.

Knowing about the life of a man in a wheelchair, helps us to understand the reason for Elvira's reaction in her mother's womb, when she felt tight and unable to move her legs. Her spirit had been trapped in those two experiences, causing her a feeling of limitation, dependence and stagnation in her current life.

After helping Elvira's spirit to understand that the limitation of her legs belonged to another body, we helped her to free herself from those events in order to eliminate all her symptoms and sensations.

At the end of the session, Elvira had a peaceful expression on her face. When she came out of the trance, she got up from the chair and hugged Petri and me, thanking us for the help. When I turned around, I saw that those who had been watching were absolutely amazed. Elvira's experience was a gift for everyone and an excellent example of what can be done when two techniques are combined.

What Else Can Be Achieved with Hypnosis?

Based on my years of experience, there are almost no limits to this spiritual tool. Despite its most common characteristics and aspects, hypnosis serves to reprogram behaviors, treat addictions, fears, phobias, and sadness, among other consequences.

As I have explained in previous pages, at the beginning of the Introspective Hypnosis sessions, I start working around a symptom of my client, without really knowing what will happen next. One of the things I have learned over the past few years is to expect the unexpected, since there is no agenda or script to follow. Even the person receiving the session does not know or have control over what will happen.

That's why a big part of the success of a session lies in being able to adapt to how the session unfolds. The limit of our clients is us. That is to say, if we allow our beliefs or prejudices to get in the way, then that is as far as our clients will go.

It is fundamental, in the type of hypnosis I practice, to focus on the spirit of the client rather than on the mind. The spirit has all the information we need to help him, and the answers to all the questions. Let's remember that it doesn't die. If we focus on the spirit who knows all those experiences, we will get the information we need to help the person. If, on the contrary, we focus only on the mind, it would be like seeing a beautiful landscape on a beach through a keyhole. How much could we really see?

Among the procedures I have tried with my clients, is that of putting two people in a trance at the same time to take them to a previous existence in which they knew each other. I was able to do this with two sisters, who met in a previous life. Each one gave me additional details about the same scene they lived.

When I saw one of Dr. Angel Escudero's videos, a practitioner and promoter of non-hypnosis thought healing, I decided to recreate his technique during a demonstration session in my Introspective Hypnosis class in Lima, Peru. At that time, Gina, of whom I spoke above, was pregnant and I arranged with her to program her body to eliminate pain at the time of delivery. The results were impressive during the class and during delivery, as she told me a few months later.

On another occasion, I was able to assist Dr. Carlos Vasquez, a dental surgeon and fellow student, who was interested in learning about the use of hypnosis as anesthesia in dental procedures.

Another technique that has generated great results and has been very well accepted by my clients, has been the telepathic session. In it, a person is put into a trance so that they can connect with another person who needs help, working through them.

Among the traumatic memories that people visit during the hypnotic trance, there are those where they have lost a loved one, either by death or simply disappeared without a trace. When this is the case, I apply the concept that time and space do not exist. This is how we try to establish communication with that spirit -whether it has reincarnated again or not- to help the client to deal with the grief and understand that what died was the body and not the spirit.

Remote Viewing

One of the cases I dealt with in my office that caught my attention was that of Nicolás, a man from Central America whose brother had disappeared several years ago. The family assumed he was dead, and I assumed the same. It was during this session that I put into practice something that I had only tried in past life regressions, where there is really nothing that can be proven.

Already in a trance and, as expected, Nicolás returned in time to the moment he received the news.

Nicolás: My mother has called me and says that my brother has not returned for a couple of days.

Antonio: You are a spirit who is in a body and your brother is too. Or he may no longer be in a body, but let's ask the universe to help us find him. I'm going to count from three to one and I want your spirit to be in the moment your brother leaves the house. I want you to connect with that moment. You are spirit, you can go back in time and visualize. Three, two, one. Look for your brother's spirit when he leaves his home. Do you see it?

N: Yes -he answered as tears streamed down his face.

A: What is happening there?

N: My brother is at the kitchen door. He's waiting for someone to come to work.

A: How is he dressed?

N: A blue shirt and gray pants.

A: Is it day or night?

N: It's daytime.

A: Go ahead until he leaves the house.

N: They've already come for him in a blue car.

A: And what happens?

N: He's leaving with that person.

A: I want your spirit to fly, to float, and to follow your brother down that road. And I want you to tell me everything you see. What's going on? Are you following them?

N: Yes, they are ahead of my town.

A: I want you to go ahead in time. Follow them. You can go faster and see if they stop at any point or what happens.

N: Some people stop them.

A: Are they civilians or police?

N: They are in black.

A: How many are there?

N: Five.

A: And what happens?

N: They are taken away.

A: Follow them. See where they are taking them. Keep floating.

N: To a farm.

A: Can you see where that farm is or how close it is?

N: No, I don't know, but it's just outside my town.

A: Is there anything you can recognize where they were stopped? Any marks, signs, or vegetation?

N: No, there's nothing.

A: Then go ahead. They are moved to the farm and what else happens?

N: They are beaten.

A: There, where you are floating, you have the gift of telepathy. Find out why they are being beaten and why they have been stopped.

N: They are standing.

A: Then go ahead and see what else is going on.

Nicolás went on to describe everything that happened that day. His brother's disappearance was definitely due to some kind of kidnapping or settling of scores. His answers to my questions were slow, as he was seeing more than I was asking him, while trying to process everything.

A: Go ahead until you find out what they do to them. What happens to your brother?

N: They get beaten up and locked up.

A: See if your brother's body is still alive.

N: It is.

Nicolás had entered the space of no time, and had been able to connect with his brother and get information about him. The session continued for a few more minutes, during which I asked him to return the same way, but this time looking for details that could indicate the location. He could see the name of the city on the road signs, names he was not familiar with, and other details. By the end of the session, Nicolás had been visibly surprised by the experience, although he did not remember everything that had happened there.

The Spirit that Helped His Daughter Remember

A few days before the Introspective Hypnosis class in Charlotte, North Carolina, Marisel, who was attending the course that would begin in a few days, had her own hypnosis session to work on various issues that she felt were still pending. One of the comments she made during the interview was that she could barely remember several years of her childhood.

Based on the studies I have conducted and my experience, I knew that when that happens it is because the conscious mind encapsulates a traumatic memory and keeps it in the subconscious until we are ready to work on it, causing a kind of amnesia in which the event is not consciously remembered. For this reason, I wrote in my notebook that I should pay special attention to the memories that Marisel might return to once in a trance.

Once the session started and in an expanded state of consciousness, she presented blockages when we tried to return to sad memories. I knew that she had experienced several difficult events, and it seemed that this was the reason she had focused on forgetting so as not to feel, so as not to be affected by them.

For several minutes, I tried to guide her into some sad event, but she simply replied that she didn't remember anything or that nothing was coming to her mind, which is impossible. We can all remember, and we have all experienced painful events in our lives. What was happening with Marisel was that her conscious mind was protecting her from them.

So, I decided to ask her to go to any memory, even a happy one if she wanted to. When I counted from five to one, Marisel traveled to her wedding day and started telling me in detail what was happening. One of the things she mentioned was that her father, who was sick and did not have much time left to live, was present. When I asked her to tell me what her father looked like, she said, "He looks and he watches, but he has a sad look on his face because he knows he doesn't have much time left". By the time of our session, her father had passed away several years ago.

I was looking for a way to return Marisel to her childhood to work through any traumatic events she might have had. The scene of her marriage made me think of communicating with her father in that memory so that he could help me. It is worth noting that Marisel quickly went into a deep trance, which allowed her to relive that memory as if it were there again.

Antonio: Three, two, one. You are already there, Marisel. Tell me what comes to your mind.

Marisel: I am dancing -she answered with a smile.

A: How old are you there?

M: Twenty-four. It is my wedding day with David. There's my dad too.

A: And how do you feel?

M: Happy, everyone is there.

A: And what else is going on?

M: Everyone is dancing and laughing. There are a lot of them. My dad is quiet, because he says he's leaving, but we're all happy.

That last sentence is what gave me a clue that there was already communication going on between the two on a spiritual level.

A: And why do you think your dad is quiet?

M: Because he's thinking that he's leaving soon.

A: And where is he going?

M: To join the universe and he's looking at me -she said with tears in his eyes.

A: Ask your daddy, since time doesn't exist and everything happens now, why he is silent.

M: Because he knows he won't see us physically anytime soon.

A: He has said a great truth. He has said physically. The body is only a biological suit that we spirits use to be on this planet. Ask your daddy to go forward in time and tell you if, once he's a spirit, he's going to be able to see you.

M: He says yes.

A: Then ask your dad, who is spirit now, how he is doing.

M: He's in the union with the universe.

A: Then, from that union with the universe, ask him if he has any advice or message for you.

M: I am always close to you -she said-, repeating what her father transmitted to her.

A: You see? Then why are you sad if he is always close to you? What we have to do is not to see only the physical body, but to feel the spirit too, the energy. Ask your father if he is aware of everything that has happened in your life since he left, since he went ahead of us.

M: He says yes.

A: And what can he tell you about your life, about the decisions you are making?

M: I am proud of you. You are doing well -she said-, repeating her father's message.

A: Would you lend him your mind and lips to communicate with me?

M: Yes.

A: I'm going to count to three and you change. Three, two, one. Change. Floyd, good night, thanks for the communication.

Floyd: Good night -he replied in a softer, more leisurely voice.

A: Floyd, I have a few questions to ask you to help Marisel. Could you answer them for me?

F: Yes -he answered, as Marisel's eyelids moved faster, indicating a deeper trance.

A: Floyd, Marisel tells me that she doesn't remember anything from her childhood until she was nine years old. However, now she mentioned two memories, one from when she was four and another from when she was five (these were happy). Do you know why she has blocked out other memories?

F: Her mother and I used to argue in front of the two girls.

A: And you think that's why she blocked out those memories?

F: Yes, because she didn't like it.

A: Floyd, tell me, are you in the light?

F: Yes.

A: And from the light, how could you help me to make Marisel remember all those years? There is valuable information that she must have about that period. We all need that part of our identity. I understand that they can be sad memories, but if we teach her to change her perception of what happened and help her withdraw that negative emotion that she felt at that moment, maybe she can remember everything else. Do you think so?

F: Yes.

Thus, Floyd helped his daughter understand why she had chosen to be born into that family and the lessons she should learn through that fact. He spoke to her about learning unconditional love, helping her to heal the wounds of the past, recover memories that had been blocked, and understand the true perception of what had happened.

Understanding the concept that time does not exist allowed Marisel to journey into a memory and to establish a communication with her deceased father in the present time, in the now.

To Young Hypnosis Practitioners and Students

To all those who already practice hypnosis in its various forms, I want to express my gratitude and admiration. I know all the sacrifice this entails, not only from you, but also from your families, as you accompany them and give them the support they need.

For those of you who are thinking of learning some of these techniques, or who are perhaps just starting out, I want to tell you not to give up. Keep going and never doubt your abilities. You can achieve anything you set your mind to.

Never forget that each one of you has been chosen for this mission and that, when you accepted it, the greater light sent you with all the necessary support and guidance. Many times, you will feel that you are not made for this work. At those times, try not to listen to your ego, but to your heart. And, whenever you wish, ask for help from your guides and beings of light. They listen to you and are there to give you a hand.

Remember that each person who comes to you will experience what they have to experience in their session, whether they like it or not. Many will not realize what they have obtained until days, weeks or months later. You did what you had to do under the guidance of the beings of light who accompany you. Do not hesitate.

Do not be afraid. There will be sessions in which you will have to help challenging spirits attached to the energy field of your clients. Treat them with love and respect. Find out their story, why they didn't go into the light, and why they got lost. Listen to them without judgment, letting them know that you are there to hear and help them no matter what they have done.

I encourage you to learn all that you can, to open your minds and your hearts, to make mistakes, and from those mistakes to learn all that you can.

Remember that the limit in a session is not defined by the person to be treated but by us, the hypnotherapists. The client will be able to go as far as our belief system allows. Do not set limits. Open your soul, heart, and mind to a new reality, a new dimension. Trust.

SPIRITS IN HYPNOSIS SESSIONS

Another rewarding aspect of hypnosis, based on the fact that we are spirits having a human experience, is being helpful to those who are lost. These spirits have not been able or willing to return to the light or source, and have remained in this dimension. Many times, they end up attaching to a person's energy field or aura, causing different physical, emotional, or mental symptoms.

In order to understand this concept, we must stay away for a moment from any idea taught by religions regarding heaven, hell, purgatory, and demons. I do not seek to convince anyone of what I will explain next, but I think it is fundamental to share with you what I have found in my hypnosis sessions, which at the same time, corrob- orates what other hypnotherapists have also mentioned. Among the most representative professionals in the world of regressive hypnosis, we have Michael Newton, Aurelio Mejía, and José Luis Cabouli, from whom I have learned and read a lot. I know there are several others, but they are the ones I identify with the most in this field because of their focus on love and forgiveness in therapy.

In my years of experience, I have encountered many different spirits during the sessions I have facilitated. Thus, I myself have been able to verify that neither hell, nor purgatory, nor demons, nor Satan exist. Although I have encountered spirits that have communicated with me through my clients by changing their voice, moving their bodies abruptly and using a threatening tone, in the end I have always managed to find out why they were attached to my clients, how their bodies died, and why they have not been able to leave for the light.

My approach when dealing with lost spirits is to help with love and respect, based on the principal that we all come from the same source. Therefore, I know that they deserve my respect and help in this hard process. On many occasions, I have not only given therapy to my clients, but also to the spirits attached to them.

Throughout my years of practice, I have come to understand that there are no good or bad spirits, only some that are more advanced than others. If any of them intend to cause us problems, they are not doing it out of evil, but out of ignorance. If they knew that in the future, they would have to experience the same thing, they would simply not do it.

There are many books that talk about the spirits. Among them is, "The Book of the Spirits," by Allan Kardec (1804 - 1869) - pseudonym of Hippolyte Léon Denizard Rivail-. In his work, the French professor and philosopher has learned the following definitions provided by advanced spirits through mediums

What is the spirit? The intelligent principle of the universe.

What is the soul? It is an incarnated spirit.

So, are souls and spirits the same thing? In fact, they are just spirits before joining the body; the soul is one of those intelligent beings that populate the invisible world and temporarily cover themselves with a carnal envelope, in order to purify and enlighten themselves.

This means that, outside the body, it takes the name of spirit, and inside the body, that of soul. The spirit is basically energy, our natural form. And, because it is energy, the spirit never dies; it only transforms. It is the spirit that decides to reincarnate in different bodies to experience the illusion of separation, of not being part of a whole, and to learn to experience emotions as well, something that can only be done through a body.

What Is a Lost Spirit?

A lost spirit is one who, for different reasons, has not returned to the source and is still on this plane. Many of them decide to adhere to the energetic body of a person, causing him/her different ailments. These are some of the reasons why they stick to another energy body:

- They have not realized that their physical body has died.
- Revenge for some dispute in this or another life.
- To stay close to loved ones.
- To continue to experience their addictions through others.
- For fear of the punishment they will receive for what they did in life.
- To give a message.
- They have been sent by others with the intention of causing trouble.

I know that there are many reasons why a spirit determines not to go into the light. Let us remember that all of us have free will and not only while on Earth, but also when we return to spirit form. It is for this reason that many choose not to return.

By not returning to the source, the spirit maintains its ego: the same personality, beliefs, addictions and characteristics it had when it was reincarnated. We can say that it is basically the same individual, but without a body. It is this personality that manifests itself through people during the trance, and influences them in their day-to-day life, causing them all kinds of problems.

The mere fact that a lost spirit attaches to our energy field, whether with good intention or not, can generate all sorts of issues for us. The spirit is energy that has conscience and, when it attaches to us, what happens is that the conscience of it interferes with ours. This manifests thoughts, emotions, or physical sensations that do not belong to us, but that we believe to be ours.

It is common to hear people who come for a session, say phrases that give me a suspicion of the true reason for what is happening to them: "Sometimes I feel I am not myself,""I hear an internal voice that tells me things,""at night I feel that something is lying on me," "I have been told that I speak in my sleep in a language that is not understood," are some expressions that I have heard my clients say. These may be indicative of a spirit attached to their energy field.

More than once I have had to facilitate a session for people diagnosed as bipolar or schizophrenic, who actually had a spirit attached to him/her, and the voices the schizophrenic heard were the thoughts the spirit transmitted to them.

It is common to hear a person say that they went to the doctor to have a physical pain treated and that, after all kinds of analysis, they couldn't find anything, but the pain was still there. Perhaps the answers can be found in a hypnosis session.

In order to facilitate the understanding of what spirits are and do, I will group them into three categories:

Our Loved Ones

These are our deceased relatives who decided to stay close to us, either to accompany us, because maybe they left us in a bad economic situation when they left, or because maybe they want to make sure we choose the right people in our lives.

This may be the case for those parents who stay on this plane looking after their children, or couples who want to look after and make sure the other one is okay.

Truly Lost Spirits

These are spirits who usually have not realized that their body has died and do not understand what is happening. This can be caused by an instantaneous death, such as a car accident, a heart attack, drug overdose, death in an operating room under general anesthesia, or people in a coma.

Basically, they are individuals who were alive and left at one time or another.

Spirits Seeking Revenge

These are spirits with whom we had some altercation in this or another life, and who, by attaching to us, seek revenge by causing all kinds of problems in our lives. These, unlike the ones grouped in the other two groups above, are aware of the damage they cause and adhere to our energetic body on purpose.

How Do Spirits Manifest Themselves?

When the client is in an expanded or altered state of consciousness it is easier to make contact with that other energy, that other consciousness attached to their energy field. It is in this state that the person can feel the pain related to how that spirit's body died. It is also usual for this to be detected when the dates provided by the client during the session are out of range, or their responses are out of context.

When doing a spiritual aura scan, some people see them as attached energies and others as shadows attached to their energy body.

What Symptoms Can Attached Spirits Cause?

Pain related to the way your body died: suicidal thoughts, sudden changes of temperament or mood, nightmares, loss of time, temporary amnesia, depression, and different emotions felt at the moment of death.

Who Is Susceptible to a Spirit Attaching to Them?

Our aura or energetic body is our protection. When we are vibrating at a low frequency, that is, when that energy field is not at one hundred percent, that is when the spirits see the opportunity and attach to us.

When can a person vibrate at a low frequency? When they have addictions, when they have suffered physical and emotional abuse during childhood, have had miscarriages, have depression, or even have had surgery with general anesthesia. It is worth mentioning that this is not a rule and it does not always happen this way.

Something I would like to make very clear is that there is no such thing as possession; that is, the displacement of our spirit by allowing another to enter our body and replace it. Spirits attach themselves to our energy field and from there interfere with us. There are cases in which their consciousness is so strong that they take temporary control of the body of the affected person, but it is not a displacement of the spirit.

The integration of the spirit that is going to reincarnate in the body of a fetus takes time. The process of connection with the brain, emotional system, and neurotransmitters is not immediate. In my Life Between Lives sessions, when taking the people into the womb, which is the first real contact with their spirit, they have reported in great detail how their spirit gradually integrated with that body, describing the complications and challenges they faced in doing so. This is why I find it hard to believe that one spirit can displace another to control its body. To this day, I have not heard a hypnotherapist with recognized experience, report such an event.

How Can We Help a Lost Spirit?

Apart from the knowledge one can and needs to have in the field of hypnotic regressions, the main ingredient is love. Then, there is also compassion and the desire to help that spirit go into the light. I think it is very important to have the gift of service and the patience to do it, understanding that it is a being that is confused, lost, and that many times has not even realized that its body has died.

Even with those who have consciously attached themselves to the person to cause problems, it is important to have patience to communicate with them and make them understand that what they are doing, more than helping them, is slowing down their spiritual evolution.

There will be times they will insult us, change their voice to frighten us, say that they are Satan, or that the person they stuck to belongs to them. We must know how to leave our ego aside and not react to what I call "special effects" in order to continue helping them.

Like all of us, every stuck spirit has a story. They have gone through difficult times and it is essential to find out and sometimes help them remember it, so they can close the cycle, work out forgiveness, and go into the light. Helping these invisible beings is rewarding and these are special moments. Many say goodbye with thanks while the client's expression in trance changes completely.

The Burned Town

To better illustrate what can cause a lost spirit to adhere to our aura, I would like to share Patricia's session. Patricia found me through Google while looking for someone who practiced hypnosis in Spanish in Charlotte, the city where I reside. Patricia didn't know anything about me, nor was she familiar with the hypnosis technique I use or the videos I have uploaded to YouTube.

During our phone conversation, I could hear the desperation in her voice. "I feel as if I'm suffocating, and I'm afraid that one day my husband will come home and find me dead," she said. Immediately, I suspected that this phrase was coming from another experience, either from another life or from a spirit influencing it, since obviously Patricia wasn't really choking.

I asked her to watch my videos on YouTube so she could become a little more familiar with what I was doing, and if she was still interested, we could schedule a session. She called me the next day to arrange one as soon as possible.

During our conversation before the session, she told me that this was something that happened to her frequently, and that it had been getting worse over time. She even felt she was suffocating during the birth of one of her children, but the doctors told her husband that the monitors did not indicate a breathing issue, and that it seemed to be an emotional symptom.

Already in a trance-like state, I asked her to go to a sad memory, one that had caused her some discomfort. When I counted from five to one, she went to one where she and her mother were working at a street stand selling Mexican snacks. As I asked her questions about that scene, she began to cough.

Patricia: I'm choking! -she said, as he made sounds with her throat.

Antonio: There with your mom? -I asked her trying to find out if the choking was in that memory or in the session.

P: Yes.

A: And why are you choking? Look at it from the outside so that it doesn't affect you. That way, you can breathe calmly. Why are you choking?

P: I'm eating.

A: Are you choking while eating?

P: Yes.

A: Does that always happen to you?

P: Yes.

A: It doesn't matter what you eat?

P: No

She had been experiencing this symptom since her adolescence. Now, my mission was to find out when it had originated.

A: I will count from three to one and ask your subconscious mind to take you to another time when the same thing has happened to you. You are spirit and can travel in time and space. Search in this life or other lives. Go to the root cause. Three, two, one. Place yourself there.

P: I'm in the field.

A: Where you are, I want you to look at your feet and tell me what you're wearing.

P: Nothing.

A: Touch your body and tell me what you're wearing.

P: A brown dress.

A: Are you young or old?

P: Young.

A: What is the name of this place you are in?

P: I don't know.

A: What color is your hair?

P: Black.

A: Do you wear something on your head?

P: A hat.

A: And what is your name?

P: I don't know.

A: And what else do you see in the field where you are?

P: Horses, many horses.

A: Are they yours?

P: No. They are running.

A: And what do you do in that place?

P: I'm scared.

A: Why?

P: Because they are running.

I continued to ask her questions about that past life and the horses she saw. She told me that they were running because they were afraid and that she was afraid of them, but I didn't know why they were afraid.

A: Do you live around there?

P: No.

A: And how did you get there?

P: I'm standing.

A: Go a little forward in time until something happens. This is the origin of your choking. What is happening?

P: There are dry trees and lots of wind. People are coming running.

A: What else is happening?

P: They are afraid.

A: Like the horses?

P: Yes. They don't see me -she said, surprised.

A: And you are standing in front of them?

P: Yes.

A: And they don't see you because they run by or what?

P: I don't know. They don't see me," she repeated.

A: What else happens?

P: There's a fire.

A: Can you smell it?

P: No, I see it. It's burning.

A: The field?

P: No, the houses.

A: Can you feel the heat?

P: No, I see it. It's my house that's burning.

A: Is it the only one that is burning or are there more?

P: There are more.

A: And what are you going to do?

P: I'm afraid -she answered, I'm alone and I'm afraid.

A: Go ahead and tell me what's happening.

P: I'm afraid.

A: What happens when you get close?

P: It's very hot.

I kept asking her questions about the house that was burning. I felt that I was getting closer to the source of her suffocation. The woman in that life was telling me that she couldn't put out the fire, and that she was outside of her house. She kept telling me over and over again that it was too hot and that she couldn't put it out.

A: What else is going on there?

P: I'm alone and I can't walk.

A: Why can't you walk?

P: I'm afraid.

A: And can you breathe?

P: No -she answered, shaking his head from side to side.

A: And why can't you breathe?

P: Because it's too hot.

A: And the people ran away?

P: Yes.

A: I want you to move forward and see what happens.

P: I can't walk and I'm afraid. I can't walk.

A: Move forward in time and tell me if you can get out of there.

P: I can't.

A: Is the fire coming?

P: Yes.

A: I want you to go ahead and tell me if that's where your body dies, go ahead. What happens?

P: It's standing there.

A: Who's standing?

P: Me.

A: What's wrong with you there?

P: I can't move. I can't breathe because the smoke won't let me.

A: Move forward and tell me if that's where that body dies. Did you get away?

P: No. I'm asleep - in reference to her body having died.

A: Did you faint?

P: I don't know.

A: Move forward until the moment you leave your body - is that where your life ends?

P: Yes.

A: What do you see when you leave your body?

P: I see a lot of smoke. My body is lying down and I see my feet and my dress burned.

Once out of the body, I helped her evaluate the reincarnation that she had just completed in order to have a better understanding of the lessons that had been presented to her. To confirm my suspicions, I asked her the following question:

A: Now that you are out of the body, what else do you see? What else is happening? Where do you decide to go, now that you are spirit?

P: To the country.

This would be the answer that would explain what was happening. When the body dies, usually the spirit goes to the light or sees other beings of light coming for it. In this case, the woman's spirit returned to the field, where she was watching people running, not seeing her, and visualizing a fire whose smoke she could not smell.

As I returned to her to the moment she was outside her house trying to put out the fire, she went from not feeling or smelling, to doing it, because until that moment, she was alive. What we can assume happened is that, because of the fire and the smoke, the woman lost consciousness and died in that place. This kind of death, in a state of unconsciousness, produced confusion in her, because when she was in the field watching the horses, she had not yet realized that her body had already died.

A: Do you see someone coming for you?

P: No.

A: Do you see any light?

P: No, I am alone. I am floating.

A: Move forward and tell me if at any time you find the light.

P: I'm not afraid anymore.

A: But you haven't gone into the light.

P: No.

A: Then I'll ask you a question: are you Patricia in a past life, or are you attached to Patricia's body?

P: I'm attached.

A: And at what point did you attach to her?

P: When she was born.

A: And why did you decide to do that?

P: Because I'm afraid.

At this point, we understood the reason for Patricia's choking symptom since she was young. In fact, that physical manifestation was not hers, but that of the woman who died, suffocated and burned in that fire. Every time Patricia faced situations where she felt fear, the symptom of the burned woman's suffocation was triggered.

After obtaining that information, I worked with that woman's spirit so that she could go back to the source, and then with Patricia so that she could forgive the spirit for the symptoms it had caused her. When she came out of the trance, she didn't remember anything that happened in the session. When I told her everything that had happened, she could not believe it. She would be even more surprised when he saw the video I recorded of her session. From that day on, Patricia did not experience any more choking.

Patricia's example and the lost spirit of that woman who had died of suffocation, is just one of the many cases I had to facilitate. From the conversation with that spirit, we can realize that behind that voice that spoke to me, there was a consciousness with fears, emotions, and a lot of confusion about what was happening. In this way I treat the spirits that manifest themselves during my sessions as the human beings they were.

Some might say that what I practice is an exorcism, that the goal of hypnotherapists is to get rid of the spirits. Nothing could be more unrealistic. When I facilitate my sessions, I do not follow any specific religion, but rather always respect the beliefs of my clients. On the other hand, I have seen that some religions label the lost spirits attached to people as demons and even ask them to go to the hell they belong to or came from.

How would a person feel when, being lost, disoriented and in need of help, she ends up being discriminated against and insulted? What reaction would we get in return? One thing I learned from Aurelio Mejía was to respect the spirits. This is exactly what I do and the first thing I teach in the courses I give when I get to the module on spiritual assistance. In the years that I have practiced hypnosis, I have never had an incident with them. I suppose it is because they can see in my aura my intention to help them with love.

FORGIVNESS THERAPY

We have previously talked about the concept of non-time. We have demonstrated through sessions that I have facilitated, how spirit doesn't understand about time. For it, everything happens now.

One of the main reasons that we human beings experience different psychosomatic symptoms, is repressed emotions, generally originating in events in which we were victims of something that we have not yet forgiven.

This can apply to past events in the present life or to past lives, although for the spirit, it is the same because it feels everything now. The reasons can be as simple as a word said by our parents, without thinking, when we were little kids, and as complicated as being killed in another reincarnation, or having suffered a rape. If we have not forgiven, we have not closed that cycle or released our energy trapped in that event. Therefore, there will be a version of us trapped in time reliving that event over and over again, causing symptoms in the present.

It is when we feel victimized that we give control of our life energy to someone else. It is this role that prevents us from taking responsibility and ownership of the event we have faced, causing us to try to validate our viewpoint over that of others without understanding why we went through that experience.

If we start from the point of view that we plan our lessons, that we also choose our parents, make contracts with our partners, children, and other individuals who will have transcendental roles in our lives when it comes to reincarnation, we may realize that victims do not exist. Rather, if we allow our spirit to embrace that experience, painful as it may be, and process it fully, it can learn the lesson that we ourselves planned before we were born, continuing our evolution.

The obstacle lies in the spiritual amnesia to which we are all exposed when we are born: forgetting who we are and why we are here. When we go through various situations that we ourselves planned, because we do not remember doing so, we allow a negative emotion to be associated with that event, thus creating a repressed emotion. Over time, this will manifest in different ways, including physical symptoms.

On the other hand, our energy will be caught up in that incident, causing our spirit to relive it over and over again, leading to the same problems mentioned above.

One thing we must remember, apart from the lessons planned in the spiritual world and the contracts we make with other spirits to be part of our reincarnation, is that when we arrive on Earth, we are affected by the wheel of karma. As I explained earlier, karma is not a punishment as is often believed, but only the law of balance. This means what we made someone else feel, will touch us with the same or greater intensity. If perhaps today we feel like victims, it may be that in another life we have been victimizers. This is only part of the evolution of our spirit.

What Is Forgiveness and How Does It Work?

We must start by understanding that forgiveness does not mean making peace with our aggressor. Nor does it mean to stop seeking justice, to maintain the bond with that person who hurt us, and much less to forget what happened. Forgiveness is making a decision to stop hurting ourselves, perhaps thinking that we are hurting our enemy.

When a person in a trance-like state goes into a memory where he felt victimized, he is guided by the hypnotherapist to change the perception of what happened; that is, the real reason for the that event, the lesson he should learn from it. Thus, the negative emotion associated with that memory disappears, erasing also the emotional or physical symptom.

In my years as a spiritual hypnosis therapist, I have witnessed how not forgiving what was done to us can have such devastating effects as developing cancer or tumors. In other cases, not forgiving has caused people to close themselves off from love and choose to live in isolation for fear of being harmed again.

I handled several cases of women who were raped and who, by not forgiving, caused that emotion and negative energy to attach to their uterus, just as a lost spirit would have done. In other words, they created their own attached spirit that would not allow them to become pregnant. I have also facilitated sessions in which only forgiveness of an event during childhood allowed for the healing of symptoms and illnesses that the client felt as an adult.

We could say then that we have total control over how we perceive what happens to us, and what emotions will be associated with that incident.

Upon careful consideration, if we created that negative association, we can disassociate it ourselves. As I have already mentioned, we cannot modify what has happened, but we can modify our perception.

The Rapist Soldier

To explain how every victim has been an aggressor at some point, either in the current reincarnation or in a previous one, I would like to talk about Meredith's session.

During the pre-session interview, Meredith mentioned that in the course of her childhood and adolescence, she had been the victim of molestation on several occasions. Without realizing it, she was revealing a pattern that had occurred in her life. When this happens, it usually means that this is a lesson to be learned, and that it can be repeated at multiple times and in different ways until it is learned.

Already in a hypnotic trance, I asked Meredith to go back in time in search of a sad memory. She went to when she was four years old and was being molested by her father. Meredith was crying desperately as she relived this event and answered my questions. My intention was to help her understand the why of that experience. Once she worked out forgiveness with her father, I asked her once again to look for another sad memory.

Meredith went to the age of nine and relived the moment when a family friend would enter her room at night to molest her. Once again, she could not hold back her crying as she recounted this event to me in horror. After working out forgiveness with this man, we moved back in time once again in search of another sad memory. Note that at no time did I ask her to search for a memory when she had been molested. Her spirit, which knows about what she needed to work on, went to those two incidents on its own.

As I counted from five to one, giving her time to find the next sad memory, Meredith shook her head from side to side. Her body became tense and rigid, and she began to tremble and cry inconsolably.

Antonio: What is happening, Meredith?

Meredith: My father's friend is in my room.

A: And what is happening?

M: He's taking off my underwear -she said, crying and screaming desperately.

A: How old are you there, Meredith?

M: Seven. Why does this keep happening to me? -she asked, bathed in tears, as if crying out for justice-. She was referring to the series of inappropriate touches she had been exposed to.

A: Let me talk to this man. One, two, three. Change. Hey, what are you doing there?

This technique is called Role Change and consists of asking the client to lend his or her mind and lips to the absent person to communicate with me. We could say that, starting from the concept that we are all one and that a part of us - our Higher Self - resides in the spiritual world, we can establish communication with that absent person on a spiritual level.

M: I'm putting my hands inside her underwear -the man replied through Meredith.

A: How old are you?

M: Sixty-two -he said in a mocking voice.

A: Aren't you ashamed? A sixty-two-year-old man with a seven-year-old girl? Can't you get a woman your own age?

M: No, my wife is dead.

At that moment, I wanted to give Meredith a chance to defend herself. I asked her to kick him between his legs and to forcefully ask him to leave her room.

A: Tell me what that man is doing now, Meredith.

M: He got up and is leaving my room.

A: Let's forgive that old fool who didn't know what he was doing. Now let's find out why this keeps happening to you. We're going
to ask your subconscious to take you back in time and space. I am
going to ask it to take you to another life, to an incident that is related
to what you are experiencing now. Five, four, three, two, one. You are
already there. Where you are, do you feel that you have a body?

M: Yes.

A: Look at your feet. What are you wearing?

M: Boots.

A: Is that body a man or a woman?

M: A man's -she answered in a loud voice-. Her personality had
changed.

A: Young or old?

M: Young.

A: What are you wearing?

M: I have a uniform.

A: What color is your uniform?

M: Blue.

A: Do you speak the same language we're talking about now?

M: Yes.

A: What's your name?

M: James.

A: James, look around. What is this place?

M: I'm on the battlefield.

A: Who are you fighting?

M: Against the Confederate soldiers.

A: How do you feel there?

M: I don't want to be here.

A: What else are you seeing in that place?

M: There are bodies everywhere.

A: Do they belong to your people?

M: Yes.

A: How do you feel there?

M: My legs hurt because we have to walk. We have to fight and I'm tired. We have to shoot innocent people. There is no reason for this.

A: I want you to walk away from this scene and go to the next scene and see what you do and what happens there. Three, two, one.

M: I have entered a house - it communicates to me with a malevolent tone.

A: And what's going on?

M: There's a woman here and she's alone.

A: And what are you going to do?

M: I've been on the battlefield for a long time and I feel lonely.

A: How old are you there?

M: Already advanced in my thirties.

A: This woman is alone. Did she invite you or did you force your way in?

M: I forced my way in.

A: What else is going on?

M: She tells me to go away and leave her alone, but I tell her no. I'm here and I want her. I tell her that I'm going to have her, -he adds with a sarcastic smile-. So I throw her down, rip off her underwear and rape her. She doesn't want to, but I'm doing it anyway and it feels good.

A: Look at her face. How does she look?

M: She's upset and sad. She's crying, but that doesn't stop me.

A: What does she say to you?

M: To get out, to stop.

A: And you listen to her?

M: No.

A: Perfect. Then finish what you're doing. What are you doing with her now? -I said, as he smiled at the pleasure he was feeling.

M: I leave her there and go.

We had found a past life in which Meredith, being a soldier, had raped a woman in search of pleasure. How many times would he have done the same during the time he was a soldier and felt alone? In that life, he had been the perpetrator making that woman feel what it was like to be raped against her will, while she cried and screamed at him to leave her. This is where karma is generated: to feel in the same or greater intensity all that we make others feel.

In Meredith's life, her spirit had to settle that debt by experiencing what the soldier made that woman feel. Note that the reaction of the woman raped by the soldier was the same as Meredith's every time she was touched improperly. After understanding this, Meredith was able to forgive, both with the woman she raped as a soldier and with the men who touched her inappropriately in this life.

Meredith had understood that she had done the same thing in a past life. How could she judge someone for doing the same thing she did? By understanding the purpose of the experience, she was able to transform the emotion associated with the events of her childhood, eliminating any physical or psychological manifestations related to them. One could say that, in one way or another, it was the information she obtained that allowed her to heal.

For forgiveness, there is no such thing as time or space. The spirit never dies, and for it, life is one with experiences in multiple physical bodies. If we have not forgiven something that happened to us in a past life and this caused a negative emotion to be associated with it, that will cause us symptoms in the future. Most likely we will bring that symptom into this life.

Sometimes, not forgiving makes us seek revenge. It is not rare to find in hypnosis sessions that a person has spent several lives trying to work forgiveness with another incarnated spirit, with whom he has an outstanding debt.

I have even found spirits attached to the energetic body of my clients, with whom they had some unresolved incident, seeking revenge and generating all kinds of problems for them. This means that forgiveness can be given or received not only when one is incarnated, but also when one is in the form of a spirit outside the body. Not forgiving can bring serious consequences to our spirit by carrying them from life to life.

The Unfaithful Woman and Forgiveness

To continue the explanation of forgiveness, I would like to refer to María's session, about which I spoke at the beginning of this book. During her session, we found three spirits attached to her: César, whose only purpose was to tell María's aunt that he had not abandoned her, and that he had been killed while traveling; the spirit of a woman who attached herself to María when she was a child; and Raúl, of whom we will speak next.

María had suffered all kinds of emotional and physical abuse from her mother, who, in retaliation for her husband - María's father - for leaving her, decided to make life impossible for her children.

During the interview, María had mentioned to me that she had been raped during her childhood by her mother's partner. Already in a trance, she went to several sad memories, where her mother was doing terrible things to her. When we found Cesar's spirit attached to her, he warned us that there were two more spirits attached to her aura. When we finished working with him, we continued with the spirit of the woman who had stuck to her at a wake, and once we were finished with her, we were ready to start working with the third and final spirit stuck to María.

> **Antonio**: María, I want you to analyze your body from where you are. You are spirit. Look at your body spiritually and tell me what you see – she touched the part of her chest where she reported feeling a lump.

> **María**: I see a bone.

> **A**: What's happening with that bone?

> **M**: I feel something horrible.

> **A**: I'm going to take this from here and bring it to your mind - this is to give the spirit a chance to express itself-. I'm taking it, I'm taking it. Let it communicate through your mind -I said to María by touching her forehead with my index finger, as her body trembled-. Brother, how long have you been with Mary?

> **R**: Many years! -he replied in a deeper tone-, and I will not leave her alone!

> **A**: No problem. No one is telling you to do anything. In your past life were you a man or a woman?

> **R**: I don't remember.

A: It doesn't matter if you were a man or a woman, you are now a spirit -I said after a few seconds of silence-. What are you doing there with María?

R: Not leaving her alone.

A: Did you know her before? Where do you know her from?

R: I don't remember.

A: No problem. Have you caused her anything voluntarily or involuntarily? Any symptoms?

R: Yes.

A: The pain here? -I asked, touching María's chest.

R: Yes.

A: Do you regret having caused it?

R: No!

A: Then tell me why you caused it to her.

R: I hate her mother!

A: Tell me who you are. Why do you hate her?

R: She hurt me so much -he replied, shaking his head from side to side and raising his voice.

A: Did she hurt you very much? Let's see, there's something I want to understand because it seems that María had problems with her mother too, and her brother too.

R: María met me.

A: María knew you?

R: Yes, she knows who I am.

A: Can I ask her?

R: No, she was very young.

A: Ah! So, you were the mother's partner?

R: Yes.

A: Now I understand.

R: I, I... - he said with a desperate tone.

A: And what happened to you? How did you move to the spiritual plane?

R: Her mother forced me!

A: Forced you to what? We are here to help you.

R: I didn't want to. I told her no.

A: Didn't want what?

R: I told her mom I didn't want to.

A: You didn't want to what?

R: Rape her! -I didn't want to! She was too young!

A: And, brother, how old were you when all that happened?

R: Twenty-four years old.

We had found Raúl, who raped María when she was just a child. She had mentioned this event to me, but we didn't have the details Raúl had given us: "her mother made me do it."

I could feel Raúl's regret and despair as he told me what he had done to María. I continued to work with the two of them trying to get him to apologize and her to forgive him so he could go into the light and she could release the energy of that event, eliminating that negative emotion that was causing several symptoms, such as the lump that had appeared in her chest.

A: Do you want María to forgive you for this?

R: Yes, she has suffered a lot because of it.

A: Perfect, let me talk to María for a moment, please -I said, as I touched her forehead with my index finger, indicating that it was time to make the change to María.

A: María, you see we have a brother there - referring to the spirit of Raúl.

M: Yes.

A: He's the one who did something to you as a child.

M: I know.

A: Do you realize that he's sorry? Do you forgive him for that ignorance? Because he didn't know what he was doing.

M: I don't know what's happening with me, but I can't. I can't.

A: I'll explain. We evolve in the spiritual world through forgiveness. As you have been able to appreciate, you have had three spirits attached to you because no one would forgive them and because they could not forgive either.

M: I don't know why I can't -she replied, moving her head from side to side-. Brother, I can't.

A: I'm going to count to three, and I want you to go to a life where you knew him. Let's see if you two know each other from before. One, two, three. Go deep into that life. Tell me if you knew him before.

M: His name is Raúl -she said with a frown. Yes, his name is Raúl.

A: Did you know him in another life?

M: Yes.

A: And did you do something to him?

M: Yes.

A: Okay, now we're getting it. Tell me what you did to him.

M: I cheated on him.

A: You cheated on him. What kind of cheating?

M: I ran away with another man -she answered, smiling.

A: So, you were a woman and you went away with someone else.

M: Yes.

A: Then you understand where his resentment comes from. Do you realize how the wheel of karma works?

María had found the karmic origin of the incident with Raúl. They had been together in a past life, where she had left him for someone else. They didn't know this on a conscious level in this life, but on a subconscious level it affected Raul's behavior, leading him to agree to rape her when she was little in this reincarnation. Let's remember that, for the spirit, time does not exist. For Raúl's spirit, that infidelity and abandonment had happened not that long ago, or what is even worse, it continued to happen if his energy was trapped in that event.

Once María understood that she had generated karma with Raúl, she was able to forgive him, helping him go into the light. María was no longer a victim. Understanding what had happened in a past life allowed her to change her perception of what had happened in her current life.

A month later, María's aunt, who made the appointment, invited me to her hometown to facilitate hypnosis sessions for other family members. On that occasion I was able to see María, who suddenly came to visit. When she came through the door, I didn't recognize her. They had to tell me that it was María. She looked happy and radiant. Finally, she felt at peace.

As we have seen in Meredith's and María's sessions, women who at one time felt victimized by others and trapped in those experiences, were in another reincarnation, victimizers who started the wheel of karma. Sooner or later, they were going to experience, in their own flesh, with the same or greater intensity, the pain they provoked.

Think of how many times we have felt victims of others, victims of destiny or of the universe, how many times we have not taken responsibility for what we have had to live through, and how many times we have blamed others for what we are experiencing.

Everything we experience is part of our learning, and we can learn both in love and in suffering. It is not possible to modify what we have lived or are living now, but we can change how we experience those events, with responsibility and embracing all the situations that the universe puts in front of us. We should remember that we ourselves choose to go through those events for our spiritual evolution.

WHAT IS A VOLUNTEER
IN THE SPIRIT WORLD?

As a noun, the word volunteer refers to a subject who decides to render a service or perform a work of his own free will, without being obliged to do so for legal, contractual, or economic reasons. From the spiritual point of view, a volunteer is a spirit who has offered to carry out a certain mission, that is, to reincarnate on this planet in order to help and serve others.

A volunteer spirit is not extraordinary, nor does it possess super powers. Many of them, seek their own spiritual evolution through helping their fellow-beings, reincarnated or not.

Dolores Cannon, in her book, "Three Waves of Volunteers," published in 2011, explains in detail how she detected these spirits through her hypnosis sessions. Her clients would unknowingly come to her to remember what they had come to do in their current reincarnation. In this research, Cannon concluded that the purpose of the three waves of volunteers was twofold: to change the energy of our planet to avoid global catastrophes, and to raise the consciousness of the human being to ascend from the new Earth to the next dimension. The term new Earth has been used by many people in a trance to refer to the energy and frequency shifts that the planet is and will continue to experience.

As far as I am concerned, through sessions with my own clients, I have found several volunteers with various missions. They felt that they had to initiate something, do important things that they could not define with words. I think that, in a way, they were sent to my office so that, through a trance-like state, they could remember what they had planned before they were born.

More than one person will wonder why, if they are volunteers, they have forgotten their purpose. I think the answer is not simple, but we will try to find some logic in all this. One of the characteristics of the earthly experience is passing through a kind of spiritual amnesia, that is, not remembering who we are or why we came. From my point of view, human beings are here to pass tests and learn; what would be the point of knowing the lesson and all the answers beforehand? If we came to work on forgiveness with someone who took our life in a past life, it would not be convenient to know that, since it would affect our learning in love and forgiveness.

On the other hand, while we wait in the womb for the moment of our birth, we do it inside a woman who has her own history, goals, fears, phobias and problems. This will not only affect us during the nine months of pregnancy, but it will also affect our behavior after birth. As José Luís Cabouli explains in his book, "Atrapamiento y Recuperación del Alma," this would be a kind of soul entrapment in the womb, where part of our energy could get trapped during that period.

Without knowing it, being inside her vibratory field, we are being affected and programmed from that moment in our mother's womb. This programming will continue even after birth through our family, society and culture. In one way or another, these traits will influence our beliefs and way of being. We must also take into account the role of the schools we will attend, where they will teach us what they think we should learn and which does not necessarily align with our reality and purpose. It is very easy for a spirit to get sidetracked by so much distraction.

I have always been amazed to see how the universe reminds, spiritually awakens, and sends messages to the volunteer spirits, through hypnosis sessions. On several occasions, people came to my office for reasons that had nothing to do with what they would experience during their session.

Dolores Cannon went one step further and categorized these volunteer spirits in waves according to their age. She wrote her book in 2011. She determined that the first wave was between 40 and 60 years old - after the launch of the nuclear bomb in 1945-. Those in the second wave comprise young people in their 20s and 30s and are characterized by their focus on helping others. These volunteers go unnoticed and have been described as sort of antennas, beacons, power generators and channels of energy. The third wave consists of the new children, who according to the American hypnotherapist, were in their teens when the book was published. They are recognized as coming with a higher level of consciousness. They are called indigo children or crystal children.

It is well known that these new children are driven by love. Their mission is to help humanity in its spiritual awakening and to raise the level of vibration of both Earth and human beings. They resist social structures and the traditional education system.

Based on what has been explained above, we can say that the goal of a volunteer is, among other things, to help us remember that we are all one, that separation, the belief that we are individual beings, is just an illusion. We are all sparks from the same source of divine light. Volunteers and all human beings should look for the answers within themselves and not outside, as we have been taught so far.

Cannon, through hundreds of hypnosis sessions with her clients, also received many references to the so-called new Earth and the elevation to the fifth dimension. Volunteer spirits seek to facilitate this transition.

I will now summarize the information received by the American writer:

- The frequency of planet Earth is changing. Our bodies are adapting to the new frequencies and our cells are receiving new instructions.
- People who die - who return to the source - reincarnate with a purpose. Dolores was told, through people in a trance, that the planet Earth is in danger. This is where the volunteers come in.
- Our purpose on this planet is to help each other raise our vibration and frequency.
- The new Earth is a matter of consciousness and new perception. We create it with our reality and thoughts.

These concepts have not appeared recently. We have been hearing them for a long time. There are even historical mentions of the new Earth.

References in the Bible:

2 Peter 3:13: *Nevertheless we, according to his promise, look for new heavens and a new earth, wherein dwelleth righteousness.*

Isaiah 65:17: *For behold, I create new heavens and a new earth, and the former things shall not be remembered or come into mind.*

Isaiah 66:22: *For as the new heavens and the new earth that I make shall remain before me, says the Lord, so shall your offspring and your name remain.*

Revelations 21:1:

[17] *Then I saw a new heaven and a new earth, for the first heaven and the first earth had passed away, and the sea was no more.*

*1 **Thessalonians** 4:13-17: After that, we who are still alive and are left will be caught up together with them in the clouds to meet the Lord in the air. And so we will be with the Lord forever.*

Many Christians, especially evangelists in the northern United States, believe in the second coming of Jesus Christ. For them, this will take place in two phases: the first will be to take away the believers, both living and dead; the second will be after seven years of tribulation on Earth.

The Mayans

When talking about the Mayans, many think of the predictions and changes that were to take place on December 21, 2012 from an apocalyptic viewpoint. They talked about the collapse of the ecology, solar storms, different catastrophes and even the change of the polarity of the Earth. But, in reality, the Mayans spoke of the beginning of a new era, of a new level of consciousness, the beginning of a new cycle in humanity. The Mayas never predicted the end of the world as such.

A Mayan era is composed of 13 cycles, called *b'aktun,* which conclude every 5,125 years. The end of the Fifth Sun period occurred on December 21, 2012, ushering in a new era of positive change for the planet and humanity.

The Hopi Indians

The Hopi are one of the many Native American cultures of the Southwestern United States. In the state of Arizona, at a place called Oraibi, there is a rock known as 'the rock of prophecy', which is said to be able to predict the fate of mankind.

The Hopi Indians believe that we are currently living in the Fourth World, but that we are on the threshold of the Fifth World or the Fifth Age, which they call 'the world of enlightenment'. For them, in each of the three previous worlds, humanity was destroyed by harmful practices and wars.

The Hopi myth has many variations, for it is an oral prophecy. The most common story is that of the Spider Grandmother - the creator of the world - who made a reed grow in the sky, emerging in the Fourth World as a small interdimensional tunnel or passage called sipapu. As the end approaches, the sipapu seems to take the Hopi to the next phase, that is, to the Fifth World.

The Hopi also speak of nine prophetic signs that would announce the end of the Fourth World. The ninth and final sign reads as follows:

"A dwelling place shall be heard in heaven on earth, which shall fall with a great crash. It will appear as a blue star. Then, after this, the ceremonies of the Hopi Indians will cease."

Many think that this prophecy is about to come true.

Through the Use of Hypnosis

The word hypnosis comes from the Greek word *hypnos*, which means god of sleep. Hypnosis is nothing more than an altered state of consciousness. That is, the person in a hypnotic trance state is conscious at all times.

In ancient Egyptian times, we find in the temples of sleep, or dream temples, the first manifestations of hypnosis -4,000 years ago- under the mandate of Imhotep, high priest of the god Ra. These temples were a kind of hospital devoted to curing ailments. Treatments ranged from chanting and meditation to placing patients in a state of hypnotic trance in order to determine the treatment to be followed through the analysis of what they believed was a dream.

Since the seventies, Brian Weiss, Michael Newton, Dolores Cannon, Aurelio Mejía, and other hypnotherapists began to receive messages and concepts from other more subtle dimensions, such as the spiritual world, through their patients in a hypnotic state. We must remember that in those times there was no Internet or social networks.

There were not many texts that spoke about the subject, or publishers interested in it. These were the reasons that led Cannon to create her own publishing house, so that she could publish her own books and those of others that spoke of metaphysical issues and alternative healing modalities.

It is noteworthy, then, that experts in the field of hypnosis received almost the same concepts at different times, locations, and languages. Dolores Cannon, in particular, received a lot of information about the new Earth and the fifth dimension, which she later captured in her texts.

An individual in a hypnotic trance is a potential medium. We must remember that Allan Kardec, founder of spiritualism, received valuable ideas from the spiritual world through mediums. It was with these concepts that he wrote "The Book of the Spirits," which remains one of the most outstanding books in this field.

With the advances in both technology and science, and due to the excessive information, both true and false, that is found on the Internet, we have become accustomed to questioning everything that comes to us. It should not surprise us then that we doubt everything we are told during hypnosis sessions, about the new Earth, about raising consciousness and about volunteers.

I confess that I myself took the position of questioning everything, be it books, audios or videos, not only since I started learning hypnosis, but even long before that. It was difficult for me to believe in anything I could not prove or recreate. In a way, that had also been my reaction in school, when the Augustinian priests taught me about the Catholic religion. I always questioned; always wanted to prove what I was asked to blindly believe. However, I also confess that, in questioning every belief that was imposed on us in a certain way, I always felt that there was something else, something that I could not explain or describe. This feeling made me doubt everything that went against this inexplicable feeling.

On the other hand, whether by chance, causality, or as a result of our research, many of us who practice some form of hypnosis regression have encountered the same type of sessions. In those, our clients relive the moment when they return to the light, to the source, after the death of the body in a previous life. And they provide us with almost the same descriptions of the spiritual world: the resting place, the guides, the spiritual group, the advice of the sages, the choice and planning of the lessons, and the next reincarnation.

The information is the same. It tells to us about the urgency of raising the vibrational level of human beings and, therefore, of the Earth. We are told that love is the answer to everything, that we have come to help each other. We are told about free will and how we ourselves choose the lessons and situations to live. Also, we have been given messages explaining that the new Earth would not be physical - from the third dimension - but from a more subtle dimension. Some of my clients have even returned to the space between lives, at the time of planning their next reincarnation, where they were volunteering themselves to help in the spiritual awakening.

We are a few hypnosis practitioners who have asked such clients if they would like to share the video of their session on the Internet, so that others can learn from it. In these videos, you can see people of different nationalities, cultures, races, and languages experiencing and explaining the same thing. The message they send us from the spiritual world invites us to love one another and to love this planet.

Without going too far, my friend and colleague, Alba Weinman, whom I met in the Quantum Healing Hypnosis Technique (QHHT) class, and with whom I have shared my learning path in the field of hypnosis, has a lot of videos with her clients. Collective hysteria? Imagination or hallucination of the person in a trance? Each of us will have to determine that. In my case, I pay more attention to the information provided by those who do not remember anything - although it is normal to remember - as it is an indication that their conscious mind did not contaminate the session, nor the information.

Ticket to the Spirit World

To give the reader a better idea of the type of concepts conveyed in a hypnosis session, I will share a segment from Marie's session. She lived in Charleston, South Carolina, three and a half hours from where I live. When she contacted me, I informed her that there were other QHHT practitioners in her area, but she insisted on doing the session with me since she felt that it was the right thing to do.

A couple of days later, she arrived at my office and, after the interview, we began the induction. I will share a segment of Marie's session, who after being in a trance for two hours, did not remember anything about what happened.

Marie entered into a deep state of consciousness easily. I noticed this because she spoke very slowly and with a low voice. It is at this level that people take a little longer than usual to answer the questions that are asked and the session usually lasts longer.

We were just finishing navigating a past life that took place in what seemed to be the Old West, in North America. In that reincarnation, she was a dancer traveling from city to city with a group of artists. During the session, she described in great detail the clothing she wore and even did not hesitate to complain about the boots she had to wear and the hot weather in that place. The landscape was arid and the buildings were made of wood. We were finishing navigating that life without arriving at the moment of death in that body, when all of a sudden, she said to me:

Marie: I'm getting ready.

Antonio: Ready for what?

M: I have a ticket for a big event.

A: Is it an event you're going to as a spectator or an artist?

M: We're being called.

A: And how do you feel about that? -I asked without clearly understanding what was happening.

M: Excited.

A: Is anyone going with you?

M: Yes, many.

A: Then it's an important event.

M: Yes, I'm in a hurry.

A: Move forward until the moment you get there and tell me what's going on.

M: A lot of people. Wow! There are a lot of people everywhere.

A: Can you tell me what's going to take place there?

M: It's a preparation meeting. Promises.

A: About what?

M: To fix, to fix things.

A: Things for whom?

M: Gaia (planet Earth) - she responded with surprise at the number of people at the meeting.

A: And all these people are meeting to talk about planet Earth?

M: Yes.

A: And why are they worried about the Earth? -I asked her as if I didn't know what we humans are doing to the planet.

M: Its beauty is being destroyed, abused -she replied-. She cries for help.

A: Do you know what year this is?

M: There is no time -she answered.

At this point, I had already realized that Marie had skipped her death in that life to go directly to the spiritual world. What she was witnessing was nothing more than a gathering of spirits in the spirit world, to see how to help Gaia, who was asking for help because it was being destroyed.

A: And how did you go from being a dancer in the Old West to being absent from time?

M: Because I'm already up there.

A: Oh, your body died then.

M: Yes, I was called to the meeting. There are people everywhere. There's no ceiling or walls.

A: And what are they talking about?

M: An announcement. They are sounding horns and trumpets.

A: And what's the plan? How are they going to help Gaia?

M: With friends. A lot of friends who aren't from here. The brothers from the stars.

A: Other planets?

M: Yes -she replied with a nod-. Fifty-seven planets.

A: And how do you plan to help?

M: With technology.

A: What is the biggest concern?

M: The ecosystem.

A: And how do you plan to help?

M: With a machine that puts in twice as much as it takes out, like a replicator, but it's not a replicator.

A: And what is your role there? Why would they call you to the meeting?

M: I build and fix things, like plants and animals.

A: And how do you do that?

M: With groups of people - other beings or spirits.

I continued the dialogue with Marie from the place of no time, in the space between lives. I asked her if there was anything else we should know about this meeting, and she said that a bright sphere had appeared. When I inquired about that sphere, she responded that it was the presence of God, the source, the creator. Marie went on to explain that those who were there were volunteers.

Marie's case is just one of many that I have facilitated over the years. It seems that she knew on a spiritual level that she had to travel a few hours to Charleston to have this experience. Not because I consider myself special or an expert in the field, but because I suppose her spirit knew that I had the techniques she needed, to obtain that experience. Everything has a reason.

In Marie's case, the message was clear and concise: The Earth needs help, because we are damaging it without thinking about future generations who will continue to learn. There are many occasions when, through our clients, advanced spirits, guides, teachers, or beings from other planets have transmitted this urgency to other colleagues and to me.

How Can Volunteers Identify with Each Other?

It would be absurd to talk about a standard or to generalize a rule. The truth is that I don't know if there is any way to explain it in words. How can we express the attraction of similar spiritual energies and frequencies? We could start by understanding that human beings possess an energy field or aura, if you want to call it that. That means that we are vibration and, as such, we have a frequency, a kind of unique signature that identifies us in other dimensions, and that allows us to find each other.

To make an analogy, let's think about the IP address that is assigned to each computer that connects to the Internet, a unique address that allows that computer to be located in any part of the world, in order to establish communication and exchange data while connected. Because it is energy and emits a frequency, we could also think of ourselves as radio stations that emit signals, which are captured by the receiver that is tuned in.

Let's remember how many times it has happened to us, that when we met a person, we immediately disliked or distrusted them without even having shared a word with them. Or, on the contrary, that someone we just met liked us and inspired in us confidence. It is true that on a spiritual level we can recognize a person we have met in a past life, but this does not happen in all cases.

I better explain this with my experience in hypnosis sessions. I still remember the day I traveled to Arkansas for the QHHT Level 2 course with Dolores Cannon. If I am not mistaken, it was the last one she taught before she passed away. I was very excited. Not only because I was going to learn more advanced techniques, but also because I was going to be able to meet a person who I admired a lot for her work and career.

There were about fifty of us in the conference room. Most were from the United States and Canada, but several had come from other countries. The energy level in the room was incredible. Although I didn't know anyone, I really felt like I had known them for a long time. There was a great atmosphere of fellowship, which was felt and commented on by other attendees.

It felt like a school class reunion, where we would meet again after years, even though we had never met before. This would be my first experience of this kind, but, many years later, by the time I began teaching hypnosis, both the attendees and my wife, Catherine, and I would feel that same connection.

Several of us who attended Dolores' course have remained in contact over the years, exchanging experiences in the field of hypnosis and encouraging each other. Sometime later, through my clients in trance and psychics, I would be convinced that they had been put on my path. Along with them, I had volunteered to help others in the process of spiritual awakening. This was also a way for us to grow and learn.

Alba Weinman, a friend and colleague I met in that class and with whom I later shared the same teachers, has become a great friend. We have both kept in touch since that time and I consider her my spiritual sister, with whom I have undertaken different projects and taught hypnosis courses in several countries.

The same thing happened sometime later when I met Genoveva Calleja, with whom I have also shared a long path. Although she was already practicing QHHT when we met, I was able to train with her when Aurelio Mejia came to Charlotte to facilitate Introspective Hypnosis sessions. It was also Genoveva who encouraged and assisted me in training on Michael Newton's Lives Between Lives technique; and she became one of my mentors during the certification process. The friendship with Alba, Genoveva and Aurelio was instantaneous. In them I recognized my spiritual companions and in Aurelio, the teacher from whom I had surely already agreed to learn in this life. To some, this may sound like a fantasy, but it is my truth.

We must take into account that human beings store in the subconscious memories, experiences, and emotions of their present and past lives. However, we are not aware that these were stored reflecting only partially what really happened. All this information is stored in a distorted way because, before being recorded in the subconscious, it went through a series of filters, such as beliefs, past experiences, and basic needs. In other words, this means that everything was stored according to our own reality.

Thus, I write this book from my own reality. And it coincides with that of many contemporary colleagues and several others who came before me. As I received the information I have shared so far, and the information I will share in the next few pages, it will be up to you to process it through your own filters. In this way, you will not only draw your own conclusions, but you might want to use these concepts as a reference for facing future situations, or as lessons that we have learned as we evolve spiritually.

Can Volunteers Forget Their Purpose?

Of course, they can. In her book "The Three Waves of Volunteers," Dolores Cannon relates the most representative cases of those who came to her for a hypnosis session, not knowing that what awaited them was to remember the work they had come to do.

As I explained at the beginning of this chapter, one of the characteristics of this planet is that our memory is erased once we are reincarnated. This is done in order to achieve a real and deep learning, through forgiveness, detachment, and love. However, during the first years of life, we have memories of our previous life that are lost as we grow up.

There are many documented cases of children who remember having another life. Several even know what their name was, where they lived, and the names of their parents from that reincarnation. Unfortunately, as the human being grows, those memories slowly dissipate. This can occur as a natural process, because society begins to envelop and mold us, or because our own parents tell us since childhood that this or that thing does not exist, making us skeptical and incredulous. It is common to hear parents tell their children that their dreams or nightmares are a product of their imagination. This is just one of many ways in which we start disconnecting from our past lives and the spiritual world.

Have you ever heard children telling stories, while referring to when they were adults? Or saying that they see people in their rooms at night? Or that they have imaginary friends that they often play with? The human being is a multidimensional being. In the first years of life, our senses are completely open. Many of us may have thought we saw energies or spirits when we were children, heard our names being called, saw deceased loved ones, or felt like someone was sitting on our bed when no one was in the room. In reality, we are all born with these abilities, but our own family, society, educational system, and religion start to block these abilities. Little by little, as we grow up, we become isolated within ourselves.

Many times, I have come across people who have special gifts-such as psychics and mediums-who reject these abilities that they were born with. I have noticed that several of them have been sent to spiritual sessions so they could remember their path, so that they understand the importance of their gifts and their mission on Earth.

Many told me that as children they were afraid just to be alone in their room at night. Some saw energies or shadows, and others heard voices. Because of their young age and lack of experience, these events were very difficult for them to understand.

This situation was further complicated when their parents did not believe them. Some were told that it was a creation of their imagination, some were forced to stay in their room arguing that what they were describing was nonsense, and others were sent to psychologists thinking they had a mental disorder. There were some cases in which the parents, based on their religion belief, sent them to priests to perform a kind of exorcism. They thought that the voices and shadows they perceived were from spirits that were possessing them. It was definitely a traumatic experience for many of them.

The book, "The Spiritual Messengers," channeled by the famous Brazilian medium, Chico Xavier, and dictated by André Luiz's spirit, explains that thousands of spirits are sent to the planet to reincarnate with psychic gifts to help communicate with the spirits of more subtle dimensions. It also explains that many of them, once reincarnated, fail in their mission for various reasons.

In the same book, the spirits who lived on Earth with these abilities reveal the reasons why they failed in their mission. A common denominator was the influence of the family environment and the discrimination to which they had been subjected.

The Medium Who Did Not Want Her Gift

A case that exemplifies very well what is described above is that of Sandra. She was a young woman with the ability to see and communicate with spirits, but who used to panic when doing so, and did not accept her gift. Her childhood had been traumatic, always feeling different from others. Whenever she felt a presence near her, she would start to breathe in an agitated way, as if she were short of breath, and her muscles would contract from the nerves.

During our initial interview, and as I do with all those who come with such gifts, I explained to her that her ability could help many spirits who were lost in this dimension and needed someone like her. I also told her that they needed help from down here because it was very difficult for spirits from higher dimensions to do so from this plane.

Despite what I told her; Sandra was still reluctant to accept it. She was afraid of the session we were going to have, but something was driving her to have them anyway. It's under these kinds of circumstances that I know something big is about to take place in a session, that something needs to be communicated. Otherwise, why would she have come to a hypnosis session if the fear was so overwhelming?

Already in a trance and after navigating a couple of memories, I asked Sandra to look for a few more.

Antonio: Now, Sandra, I want you to move through time and space in search of another sad memory. Five, four, three, two, one You are already there. The first thing that comes to your mind.

Sandra: Nothing -she answered very sharply.

A: That means there are no more sad memories. That's good! So, I'm going to count from five to one and I want you to go to that moment in your childhood where you saw that figure of fire sitting in your room - this was something I had talked about during our interview-. Five, four, three, two, one. You are already there. In that memory, is it day or night?

S: At night.

A: What is happening?

S: I'm lying in my room. I open my eyes and there is a figure of fire sitting at the foot of my bed.

A: How do you feel there?

S: Scared.

A: Has that figure done anything to you?

S: No, it just sits there quietly.

A: Then there's no reason to be scared. If he had wanted to do something to you, he would have done it already. The best way to find out what he's doing there is to ask him. Ask that figure who he is and what he's doing there, and he will communicate with you mentally. You tell me what it says.

S: It doesn't say anything. He doesn't have a mouth.

A: No, he's not going to talk to you. He's going to communicate through your mind. That which you see is an energy. Tell me what comes to your mind.

S: A demon.

A: Very good. Then ask that demon why it's there. What does it tell you?

S: Nothing.

A: Do you want to lend him your mind and your lips so that I can communicate with him?

S: No! -she answered, shaking his head from side to side.

A: So, what do you want to tell him? If he were a demon, he would have done something to you already; besides, demons do not exist. There are only spirits, some more advanced than others. Ask him not to appear in your bed because, since you do not understand what is happening, you become restless.

S: He tells me to take care of myself.

A: See! You see? If it were a demon, it wouldn't ask you to take care of yourself. He's saying goodbye.

I noticed that Sandra was starting to breathe faster. Tears began to flow from her eyes.

S: It scares me.

A: Don't be scared. I'll explain. Those energies can visualize your aura and that's why they know you can see them. And because they know that you have this gift, they look for you to communicate. Have any of them ever done anything to you?

S: No

A: Right, they would have done something to you already. That spirit has told you something nice, to take care of yourself. An evil spirit would not say something like that. Ask him who he is and what message he wants to give you.

S: My grandfather -she said with tears running down her cheeks.

A: Very good, wonderful. Since your grandfather is there and communication has opened up, ask him what message he wants to give you.

S: He says me he wants to meet me -she said crying.

At that point, she started a dialogue with his grandfather to find out why he was there and what he wanted to communicate to her.

A: Grandpa, thank you for the communication. You know what path your granddaughter is going to start on. What advice do you want to give her today?

S: Don't trust everything, trust your heart, and don't be afraid to listen.

A: Grandpa, can you tell your granddaughter why she shouldn't be afraid to listen?

S: Because they are good energies.

A: You can tell her what to do with that gift of being able to see good energies.

S: Trust.

A: Grandpa, do you know why your granddaughter chose this gift in this reincarnation?

S: Because she is strong.

A: Should she start helping others in that way?

S: Yes.

A: Imagine how many lost souls there are that have not even realized that their body has died. Shouldn't your granddaughter help them then?

S: Yes.

This is how Grandpa showed himself to his granddaughter, sitting at the foot of her bed to give her this message. Her initial fear gave her a bad sense of what was really going on. Her fear and beliefs had caused her to see Grandpa's energy as something negative, like a demon. Once she was able to overcome the fear, Grandpa was able to communicate with her and give her the calm she needed.

I asked her to go in search of another past experience, not knowing what was about to take place. I am sure that what took place a few minutes later changed her life and her boyfriend's forever.

Sandra came to a memory where it was daytime and she was sleeping alone at home. She informed me that she was not sure if she was completely asleep, but she was on the floor. The next thing she described was that a very strong yellow light appeared. She tried to open her eyes, but couldn't. The light told her to calm down, that she had to let go and that it was God.

A: Right there where you are, I want you to imagine coming out of your body because you are spirit. I want you to go floating to one of the corners of the room and while you're floating, see everything that's happening from there. What's happening, what or who is with you there?

S: There's a lot of light in the whole room and you can see something lying there and floating above me. It's white.

A: The light is always good, and the darker the tone, the more advanced it is. Ask that light who it is and why it's there. Tell me what comes into your mind.

S: A child.

A: Ask that child why he or she is looking for you.

S: He's lost.

A: Ask that child what happened to him. How did his body die?

S: It doesn't tell me anything.

A: Then ask him not to tell you, but to show you. That child can put an image in your mind and show you how his body died.

S: Asleep

A: You mean he didn't notice when he died?

S: He didn't notice.

A: Ask him if he knows why the body died.

S: He was sick - she started breathing heavily.

A: Ask him how you can help him.

Sandra began to cry. The communication with this spirit was causing her many emotions. I tried to calm her down so she could continue. In spite of my words, she was having a hard time staying calm and started crying even more.

S: He is my boyfriend's brother.

A: So, it's okay, don't worry. He's looking for you because of that. Ask him what he wants to say to your boyfriend. I just want you to repeat what he says. Disconnect those feelings and emotions because they are not yours. How can we help him? Why is he looking for you?

S: I don't understand -she answered, shaking her head from side to side.

A: You just repeat. Don't try to understand. Do you want me to ask him and you repeat? What's his name?

S: I don't know.

A: Brother, you can go ahead communicate now -I said, touching Sandra's forehead as if to start a conversation-. Why are you looking for Sandra?

S: He says he needs help to get his brother - Sandra's boyfriend - to close the chapter of his death.

A: I see, so your brother hasn't closed the chapter of your death.

S: No.

A: How did your body die?

S: From an illness.

A: So, to help your brother close that chapter, what message do you want to give him?

S: That he shouldn't feel guilty.

A: Why does he feel guilty?

S: Because, being his older brother, he thinks he could have helped him with something.

A: That is, he doesn't accept that we leave when it's our time to leave, when we complete our cycle.

S: He doesn't accept it.

A: So that he can validate the message, can you tell him something that only you and he knew, a word, a memory or an anecdote? So that he can verify that he is receiving this message from you and can close the chapter.

S: That I am as free as the hummingbird.

A: Does he know what that means?

S: Yes.

Sandra's session continued for a few more minutes. When she came out of the trance, she didn't remember anything that had taken place, including communicating with the spirit of her boyfriend's brother. As I asked her questions about him, I realized what an incredible event I had witnessed. This would confirm to me once again that the spirit does not understand time and that in the more subtle dimensions, they have access to much more information.

The extraordinary thing about the event with this spirit was that it had taken place five years ago, when Sandra had not yet met her boyfriend. This was incredible. The brother's spirit knew that in the future she and his brother were going to be a couple, and that's why he approached her to give her the message.

Why had Sandra come to this session? What was she supposed to get? I think that was the answer. She had come, among other things, to retrieve the message that her boyfriend's younger brother had given her to help him close the cycle of his death.

Sandra was surprised and, as we talked, she tried to make sense of everything that had happened during her hypnotic trance. I think that day she understood how valuable it was to embrace her gift as a medium, to serve as a bridge between incarnate and disincarnate beings, and to help them close chapters and continue their evolution.

Just like Sandra's session, there were many more before and after her that prove that when we reincarnate, our memory is erased. This is one of the factors that make life on this planet so complicated and that, when coming, volunteers get confused or lost in the journey. To this we must add the challenge of being born into cultures where talking about these subjects is taboo, or prohibited by religion or society. Remember that we are spirits in a body, not a body with a spirit.

A volunteer spirit comes to learn its own lessons and to face all kinds of events, such as its fears, and to trust its abilities. As we saw in Sandra's case, it is easy to understand why many get confused and lose their way.

The volunteer must pass these tests in order to be able to empathize with others. It happens to me too. When I stop to discuss the issues my clients want to address in a session, and they tell me what they have experienced, I compare it to my own experiences. I see that, in a way, what I felt or thought at that moment is similar to the emotion they express. Therefore, it is easier for me to guide people, to ask the right questions using my experiences as a point of reference, although I am aware that every experience is unique.

For a long time, I believed that the fact that my life experience helped in the healing of others was pure coincidence. To my surprise, when I exchanged experiences with other colleagues, they recounted similar passages of suffering and emotions as I did, and therefore with similar learning. We had all overcome difficult moments where we felt lost and disoriented. The universe had split us in two, but little by little, we were finding our essence, waking up spiritually and remembering that we are in a school. Once these facts were understood and overcome, the phase of helping the other could begin.

The Path of a Spiritual Volunteer Is a Lonely One

One of the obstacles I have faced on this long path is loneliness. This does not mean that I have been alone along the way. On the contrary, I have always been accompanied. But it was impossible for me to talk about metaphysical or reincarnation topics with just anyone, because, as it happened many times within my family circle, they thought I was crazy. This is why I had to adopt and maintain, in a way, two identities.

Esotericism always caught my attention. Since I was a child, I felt that there was something beyond what my parents and the priests taught me at school. I never hesitated to question the teachings, ask for more information, or express my opinion, if in any case the lessons had no meaning, basis, or foundation. It was this attitude that got me into trouble more than once.

As I grew up, I was exposed to metaphysical topics thanks to my father. I remember when he told me about the book, "Many Lives Many Teachers," where the author, Brian Weiss, shared how he had discovered past lives through hypnosis. At the time, I didn't pay much attention to detail. But, when my father told me about reincarnation, despite witnessing other people's reactions to these concepts, I felt that it made total sense. Some were frightened; others, feeling their religious beliefs questioned, did not hesitate to attack him, and several preferred to withdraw and not listen to him anymore.

During a conversation with my father, while writing this book, I asked him why he had stopped reading metaphysical material, as I remembered how much he loved these subjects. He answered that he had grown tired of people making fun of him and calling him crazy and ignorant. This happened in the eighties, when we lived in Peru. If there was one thing he had learned, it was that not everyone is prepared to hear about concepts, principles, and teachings that their religion or culture has not presented to them or allowed them to believe. In the face of such scenarios, it was better to keep quiet.

The funny thing is that it doesn't matter if people in your same circle think or engage in the same thinking as you do, such as hypnosis and regressions to past lives. Everyone will end up taking their own path. Everyone works in their own way with different techniques, learning at their own pace. A great example are my friends Alba Weinman and Genoveva Calleja, two colleagues I met when I learned the Quantum Healing Hypnosis Technique. The three of us were trained by the same teachers -Dolores Cannon and Aurelio Mejia- but, over time, each one of us developed our own style. However, over the years, we have always found a way to stay in touch, share our experiences and continue learning together.

Another challenge I faced was convincing my family that there was nothing wrong with what I was doing. Today I remember with a smile when my uncles and cousins used to call me "the sorcerer" after learning that I had learned to read the Egyptian tarot, a tool that helped me tremendously to develop my intuition and perception. When, by fate, I became friends with a curandero (shaman) in Peru, my family was concerned. They thought I had gone crazy. At that time, I was about 24 years old and was just beginning to learn that there were other realities and dimensions, something beyond what our eyes could see: the spiritual world.

Several years later, I told my mother that I was learning hypnosis. I clearly remember her opening her eyes wide and saying, "What are you getting into now, my son? Be very careful." This was to be expected. She is a Catholic woman of unwavering faith. At that moment, she felt that what I was doing was against God and her religion.

When I started on this path, there were some who decided to walk away and turn their backs on me, but in return, many others arrived who were vibrating at the same frequency as I was. Lucho, a good friend that I knew before learning hypnosis, was one of those who distanced himself when he learned about the type of sessions I encountered while practicing. He ended our friendship because he thought I was engaging in the occult. So great was his fear of the unknown that he decided not to visit my house anymore and forbade his son to frequent mine, because he said that the energy of my home was heavy and plagued by spirits. If he knew that there were unseen spirits everywhere and all the time, he wouldn't have been so afraid of them.

It would not be until several years later that my family and others in my social circle would begin to believe in the possibility of the existence of reincarnation. This was made possible by the videos of the sessions that my clients allowed me to share on YouTube. Seeing these testimonies, many began to understand that there was something beyond, something they could not understand, but that in one way or another was causing positive changes in the lives of others.

IDENTITY AND THE SEARCH
FOR THE UNKNOWN

As we have read above and as described by Brian Weiss, Michael Newton, and Dolores Cannon in their books, when we reincarnate on this planet, we are not allowed to remember our past lives. That's why the term "spiritual awakening" is used to refer to when we remember who we are and why we are here.

The Farmer and the Law of Balance

One of the sessions that best illustrates this concept and its particularities is that of Giselle, which I touched upon earlier when I spoke about karma. On one of our trips to Lima and after meeting her friend from school, my wife, Catherine, asked me if there was a possibility of facilitating a session for her. I met Giselle when I was 19 years old, at the time I started to date my wife, and I knew that she had had many problems with her mother.

It had been a few years since her mother had been bedridden as a result of a blow to the head from a fall. Her situation had gradually worsened to the point where she was unable to move normally. She was like a baby in the body of an older woman who needed constant attention. As a result, Giselle had almost no social life, as she would not leave her mother alone despite having a private nurse. This caused her a lot of stress and suffering, as the relationship between them had not been the best.

I remember that during the interview, Giselle did not stop talking. Her nervousness was evident. It is usually during this time that I begin to use my hypnotic voice - a calm, paused, monotonous one - to bring my client to a state of tranquility.

She went into a deep trance very quickly. During the session, Giselle discovered that, in another life, her mother - who in that reincarnation was her daughter - had taken care of her before she died. In that life, Giselle had been a farmer named Miguel and a proud father. Now, it was her turn to return that act of love to her mother. After understanding the law of balance, we embarked on the moment of the death of that male body.

Antonio: Miguel, I want you to go to the last moment of that life. What is happening? -I asked as Giselle moved her eyes as if scanning the scene.

Miguel: I'm sick.

A: And what is happening to you? What part of your body is bothering you?

M: My body hurts horribly.

A: Do you feel weak?

M: Yes, it's an unbearable pain -he answered, grimacing in pain.

A: Where are you?

M: In bed.

A: Is there anyone else with you?

M: Yes, my wife and daughters. They are praying. They are sad.

A: Let's move to the moment you leave that body. Once that happens, tell me what you see.

M: I don't like what I see -he said in a sad voice and expression.

A: What do you see?

M: They're crying. I see my body from above. They're crying! They're hugging me! -I feel as if something is pulling me out of there.

A: Get out of the body. You are a spirit -I told him as I touched his forehead.

M: I don't feel pain anymore. I feel peace and that I can fly everywhere like a bird.

A: Looking at the life that just ended, what do you think you had to learn?

M: To take care of my body. It was a happy life, but I didn't take care of my body.

In that life, Giselle (Miguel) was able to experience the love and care of her family until the moment of her death. When I asked her spirit to give her advice for this life, it told her to stop smoking and protect her body.

It seems that Giselle was repeating the same lesson that, in a way, had not been learned in Miguel's life. I am sure she was shown that life for three reasons. First, it was important for her to remember that she had had a happy life. Her current reincarnation, full of challenges and sorrows, was only part of her spiritual learning and evolution. Second, Giselle cannot have children in this life and that causes her grief and sadness. Throughout Miguel's life, she was able to remember what it was like to have children and the excitement of seeing his grandchildren born. Finally, through Miguel's life she was able to have a better understanding of why Giselle has gone through and continues to go through difficult circumstances with her mother. This is basically karma. It is not punishment as many people believe, but the law of balance. In Miguel's life, he was given care and love while he was sick. Now it was his turn to give the same to those who did that for him.

What would happen if Giselle remembered on a conscious level the life of Miguel? If she remembered that her daughter was now her mother? How would knowing all the situations she was going to face through her mother have affected her in her childhood? The answers may be multiple as there is no absolute truth. But what I am sure of is that it would have been very difficult for her to achieve real learning, since all that information would have caused her a lot of confusion. From that day on, Giselle was able to step out of her victim role, understanding that she herself had chosen the current lessons.

It is not my intention that my answers be interpreted as absolute truth. This is a personal interpretation based on the experiences of my clients. Coming to this world remembering our past lives, the lessons we have planned in the spiritual world, the contracts we have made with other spirits that will be part of our life, and the karma we will have to pay, could cause confusion, anguish, fear and even pain.

The goal of our spirit is to learn the lessons that have been planned. Therefore, when we arrive on this planet, we should aim to remember who we really are and why we came. Every time we are faced with a sad or complicated event, instead of asking ourselves why this is happening to us, we should ask ourselves why this is happening, and what it is that we should learn from it.

It is the opportunity to take responsibility for our lives and understand that we are not victims. Many of the situations we face ourselves, we chose before we reincarnated, for our own spiritual evolution.

Going back to what I explained at the beginning of this chapter, one of the biggest challenges of reincarnating on this planet is to remember who we are, our identity. Since I was a child, I liked to analyze everything that was happening around me. Growing up in a family with several uncles and cousins on my parents' side, I had an enriching experience in the field of interpersonal relationships. Since I was a child, I had in front of me all sorts of examples of what worked and what did not work in human behavior, of course seen in a limited way due to my young age. Each one of my loved ones was a world apart, a different reality, that allowed me to learn a lot.

I remember that I could easily detect the patterns in each one of them, and thus know the test they would face in this life. Of course, not knowing anything about reincarnation, I did not see it from a past life perspective. I was only able to arrive at that analysis many years later. As a child, I thought that this was a normal process that everyone should go through, but little by little I realized that this was not the case. In time, I would understand that what was obvious to me, what I saw in the patterns of behavior that could lead to success or failure, went unnoticed by others.

In a way, I always felt different. By this, I don't mean feeling special, better, or superior to others; I was simply trying to see everything from another perspective. One anecdote that may exemplify the way others perceived me was the day an aunt showed me a caricature of a young man, whose title was *The Inquirer*. "That's you," she said. Well, yes, that was me. I asked, analyzed, and questioned everything I saw, everything I was told, and even what I was forced to believe.

It would be during my adolescence that I would begin an exploration of my identity; not so much as a human being, but as a spirit. This search for the unknown, as I call this process, became more pronounced during my youth because of metaphysical concepts I had learned from my father.

FAMILY AND SOCIAL ENVIRONMENT

One of the factors that greatly influences the search for our identity is the family in which we are born, since each family is a universe. From the psychological point of view, the family is the one that provides the child with a loving education and it is where the skills needed to be part of society are developed.

While it is true that in the family environment one receives the economic needs of food and clothing, it is also here that we find emotional support, learning our principles and values, as well as our belief system. It is during childhood that many of us will accumulate traumas and negative associations in our subconscious because the critical mind, the one that serves as the guardian of our subconscious, is not yet fully developed.

It is in our childhood and adolescence that we begin to mentally store everything that will help or limit us when we reach adulthood. If we see planet Earth as one of the many schools in the universe, then we will understand that, in addition to our family circle, there is also the country where we were born. Each country with its own religion, culture and customs will inevitably influence and condition our spiritual awakening: to understand who we are, what we came for and where we are going.

Life Is a Play

Previously, I explained the process of choosing the life, teachings, and body that we will have when we reincarnate. There is a whole procedure of planning in the spiritual world; of contracts with other spirits, which will play a special role in our life; of lessons we will learn by experiencing different situations - in love and in suffering; and of choosing our parents and the country where we will reincarnate.

We can look at life as a play tailored to our spiritual evolution. Through each main or secondary actor, we will learn something. There will be some who teach us through love, through positive and enriching situations. And there will be others from whom we will learn through suffering. It is this feeling which will act as an amplifier of that learning.

The difficult thing for human beings is to realize that we live in a play. If someone made us or is making us suffer, it is simply because we agreed with them before we returned to Earth. Surely, it was because our spirit needed to experience through that specific event. This must always be seen with eyes of love and forgiveness.

The difficulty of not remembering our past lives and who we were, added to the beliefs or blockages obtained during our growth, is what makes us feel victims of other people, situations, or simply destiny. It makes us feel trapped, blaming others for everything that happens to us. This only ruins the opportunity we have been given to learn through these circumstances. The universe knows so much about the knowledge we must cultivate that when we choose to ignore it or escape from it, it sends it to us disguised in another context. It is here that we will see the patterns that occur in the lives of certain people, that is, the same situation over and over again at different times and with other people.

Therefore, it is not uncommon to see people who always seem to face the same kind of problems: destructive relationships, abusive partners, supposed bad luck in finances, addiction problems, and problems with children, among others.

Similarly, it is not uncommon to hear those same people complain about their bad luck, blaming fate and others for what happens to them. This attitude will only end up leading them into a state of denial and deep depression. For example, if a child does not want to take the language course anymore because it is difficult for him, we know that sooner or later he will have to repeat the year and will end up taking the course again, since that knowledge will be necessary for him to solve situations when he is older.

By feeling like victims, we are simply giving our power and energy to others. By not taking awareness and responsibility for what we have come to learn, we are giving control of our lives to someone else. To prevent this from happening, when going through a difficult circumstance, let's ask ourselves what we have to learn from it. In this way, we will realize that once we have learned the lesson, the same kind of situation will not arise again.

Planning the Lessons

To better explain the concept of the play, I will tell you about Luz's case. Almost a year after his first visit, Aurelio Mejia returned to Charlotte. This time, we had scheduled about thirty hypnosis sessions for the next six days. One of them had been scheduled for a young woman. This was not only an opportunity to continue learning his technique, but also to get answers to the questions that had come up in me over the years of practicing it.

Luz was a mother of Mexican origin, very modest and with a sweet expression, who arrived at the appointment accompanied by her husband. Both were simple and noble people. You could feel a pleasant energy when you were close to them.

One of the points to discuss was the sadness she'd had in her heart since she was five years old, when her mother abandoned her and her brother. Her mother left home, leaving them both in the care of their father. This event caused her great sadness. You could see in her eyes the expression of a person who did not understand how a mother had been capable of such a thing. In the care of her father and other relatives, she and her brother had gone through very difficult times.

What I sensed -maybe I was mistaken- was that this sadness for the absence of her mother, did not allow her to fully enjoy her own motherhood experience. She had a disconsolate expression when she told us about her life.

Once the session began, we noticed that Luz was one of those people who quickly went into a deep trance. Aurelio asked her to look for sad memories in her subconscious, while he counted from one to five. While she was recounting what she was experiencing in the past, he used his techniques to help her change her perception of what had happened. Thus, he was able to remove the negative emotions associated with various events.

Seeing the ease with which Luz visualized and relived those past scenes, I dared to ask Aurelio's permission to take control of the session for a moment.

Something I usually do when a client is in a deep trance, as long as the conditions are right, is to try to bring them to the spirit world, at the moment they were planning their next reincarnation. As you read the dialogue with her during that meeting, you will understand why.

Something told me -by this I mean that, by that time, I had learned to connect with my guide and my clients' guide to proceed according to the information they provided- that I should take her to the spirit world, to the planning stage of reincarnation as Luz. I wanted her to see and remember for herself the lessons she had chosen for her current life.

Antonio: Luz, you are a spirit that has reincarnated on this planet to experience, to learn. I want you to travel in time and space, to go back, to place yourself in the spirit world at the moment before you were born. Ask the light and your guide for permission.

Luz: I see something dark.

A: How do you feel there?

L: I am afraid -she answered in a trembling voice.

A: It's all right, I'm with you. Keep moving forward and look for the light. You are changing dimensions.

L: I don't want to go.

A: Let's ask your guide to accompany you. Do you feel that you have a body there?

L: No.

From what she described to me, I could see that she was outside of the body, in another dimension where time and space don't exist.

I asked her to go ahead to the moment she was meeting with her spiritual group, planning reincarnation as Light.

A: Three, two, one. Stand there. Are you there already? -I asked after a few seconds.

L: Yes

A: Is your guide with you?

L: He is here.

A: What does he look like?

L: He is pretty, purple in color.

As Michael Newton explains in his book, the more advanced the spirit, the darker the color of its energy.

Luz was already in the spirit world with her guide and her group. She reported five spirits and was able to locate, without any problem, who her parents, brother and husband would be.

> **A**: I am going to touch your forehead and you are going to go to the moment where you plan what you are going to do in this life. What is it that you have to learn in the life that you are going to have as Luz?

> **L**: To help.

> **A**: Let me ask you Luz, have you chosen those who are going to be your parents?

> L: I chose them.

> **A**: Do you know what is going to happen with your mother when you are five years old?

> **L**: She stays, I go -she answered in a sad voice.

> **A**: Is that separation part of the learning that you have chosen for your spirit?

> **L**: Yes -she answered in a firm voice.

The session continued for several more minutes. We were able to have a greater understanding of her relationship with others in her spiritual group and to meet those who also reincarnated in this life and the role they played in it.

During the trance, her spirit guide had given her advice, had answered our questions, and was very clear in describing what she should not forget while living her life as Luz. She worked on forgiveness and was able to have a better understanding of who she was and what she had come for. Her role as a victim had culminated in her understanding that she had chosen her lessons herself and had made that contract with her mother before she was born. Now, she felt empowered. What had seemed tragic and sad had become a beautiful teaching, which had allowed her to evolve and become independent, as well as an excellent mother.

When we finished the session, Luz had completely lost track of time. She didn't know how long she had been in a trance, in fact, she didn't remember anything that had taken place. This totally validated the experience for her. She was surprised and confused at the same time, because she could not believe what had just happened.

This was just one of many sessions in which my clients experienced and reported the same thing. Their descriptions of how they visualize spirits, the color of their energy, the appearance of the guides, the number of spirits in their group. Everything matched, and not only in my clients' stories, but also in the books I had read and studied. The difference is that many of the clients had no knowledge of these books. Many of them did not even have a grasp of the concept of spirituality. They only came to a session because they wanted to feel better, because they wanted to relieve their suffering or their symptoms.

Luz's session, and many more that I would facilitate in the future, would only confirm what I have mentioned above: our life is a play tailored to our own spiritual evolution. I am sure that after her session, Luz stopped feeling like a victim of life and destiny, and that she began to see life from another perspective; wondering what she should learn from every complicated situation that had happened and was going to happen in the future. Luz had simply awakened spiritually. She had taken control of her energy and her learning.

This is only one of the sessions I mention in this book, but the truth is that many of my clients have been able to find the reason why this or that person is or was present in their life, and the reason why they had to experience difficult situations. These "villains" were actually a kind of actor who had agreed to play a role in their play to help them learn about love, forgiveness, non-judgment, detachment, and other principles.

So, I wonder, if what we experience through others is something we had already planned before we were born, why then does remembering those events produce sadness, hate and resentment? It is coincidentally this perception that we must change in our lives, for once we do, the events will not be so painful, and the emotion associated with them will be transformed. This can make the symptoms go away and the learning smoother and deeper.

PREPARATION

If we all choose the situations we will go through in our next life, I would not be free from that rule either. If I look back in time and analyze every event I have experienced -whether sad or joyful- I realize that, in fact, all along I was in constant preparation for what was to come and for what I would do in the future.

Many times, people have assumed that this process should have been a little easier for me because I already handled the concepts of spirituality and reincarnation. Why would they send me through so many trials if I was already "coming" with all the answers? On the other hand, how could I empathize with my clients and their experiences if I had not experienced these emotions myself? And finally, why would I be free from all the emotions we experience on this planet?

My life may not have been as complicated as that of my clients, who have usually gone through extremely traumatic events. But what I can say is, during the most difficult times I have experienced, I have felt lost, disoriented, and confused. As is the case with many of us, I also thought I was a victim, I felt that what was happening to me was not fair, and I blamed others for what was happening to me.

I don't consider myself special. This is why I was no stranger to the amnesia we are all exposed to when we are born on Earth. Obviously, at that time, I did not have the concepts of spirituality that I have today. That is why it was very difficult for me to understand the purpose of the situations that I experienced in different stages of my life.

What I have to admit is that, in a subtle way, my Higher Self has always transmitted to me spiritual concepts that, surely, I had already handled in other reincarnations. To explain it in a simpler way, I could say that they were like flashes of spirituality and of the preparation I should have for when it was my turn to assume the role for which I had offered myself.

I still remember as if it were yesterday, the day my paternal grandfather passed away. I was thirteen years old at the time. Without any fear and with a strange calm, I approached the bed where his lifeless body lay. I still remember the strangeness I felt when I saw my father, cousins and uncles crying inconsolably. Of course, such a reaction is completely normal when you lose a loved one, but, for some reason, my spirit was processing the event in a different way. If I took it that way, it was because my grandfather died at age eighty-two after his health broke down. The doctors had told my uncles to be prepared; however, their response to his death was as if they expected my grandfather to live forever. The thought of never seeing him again was very hard on everyone. The strange thing was that I didn't shed a single tear, and everyone noticed that. Of course, I was sad. I grew up very close to my grandfather, but I think that, deep down, my Higher Self knew that death was just a transition that we have been through many times before, and that the spirit is eternal.

Today, at fifty-two years of age, I realize that despite feeling lost and aimless in the past, I had certain constants. Although I could not describe it at the time, I was always in search of something else, something that went beyond what my senses perceived or what my religion allowed me to believe. On the other hand, in those periods of total darkness, I always found support. The universe took it upon itself to put people in my path at the right time who, in one way or another, helped me to get up and align myself with the direction I needed to go. In addition, I was always exposed to metaphysical topics and, therefore, I was in a constant search for that knowledge. Through my father, as well as other people whom I consider my teachers in different stages of my life, I was open to other realities and concepts. The universe also took care of sending me messages through people who appeared out of nowhere. It is strange to explain but, somehow, I knew they were being used for that purpose. Later, it would be through psychics and my own clients in a trance, that I would receive more detailed information, advice, and instructions from light beings, spirit guides, and the lost souls attached to my clients. These messages not only warned me of what was to come in the future, but also of the corrections I would have to make in my walk to get where I needed to be: to practice and teach hypnosis.

Everything Was Planned

As I explained above - not only based on the books I have read, but also on my clients' experiences - we plan the life we will have in our next reincarnation in detail, as if it were a play. This ranges from the choice of our parents, lessons, the karma we will have to pay, to the contracts with other spirits that will play a specific role in our lives.

The interesting thing is that, in this play, the roles of the actors are interconnected in such a way that we all learn and evolve at the same time. Like all of us, in my play there are many characters, who have had or still have a specific function. In the same way, I have a role in their play.

We could start with the beginning of my life, mentioning my parents Rosa María and Antonio, and my brother Vitor, who arrived four years after my birth. My childhood was full of love and family unity. We were not wealthy, but we lived with comfort. It was not until the early years of my youth that I experienced such shortcomings. My paternal grandfather, Tomasso, was Italian and followed his cultural customs, learned at the hands of my grandmother Mercedes. We were a typical family, including my father's five brothers with their respective families.

On my mother's side were my grandparents Rosa and Federico, and my other five uncles and aunts with their partners and children. It is not difficult to imagine that I grew up surrounded by very diverse people, who brought into my life joys and sorrows. Many family gatherings included live music, but also misunderstandings. Everything one can imagine being part of a large family. Undoubtedly, all of them were my first big school, where before any challenge that life put to us, love and union always prevailed.

My parents were my first teachers. From my mother, I learned and continue to learn about service to others, tolerance, understanding, and compassion. From my father, tenacity, how to be a fighter, and to never let go or give up. From both of them I understood that it did not matter what obstacles we encountered, as long as we were together.

My life was full of sports activities, rules to follow and strict discipline. On my mother's side, I received a lot of education in the Catholic religion. In school, a space that was never to my liking, I was an average student. There I felt pigeonholed or locked up like in a military barracks. I was always characterized by questioning everything that was imposed on me. I recognize that I was very rebellious and that I only followed the advice or teachings that resonated with me.

During my childhood, adolescence, and early youth, my father also became my friend and confidant. I am sure I am not wrong in saying that my brother felt the same way. Already in college, I met Catherine, who later became my wife and mother of my three children, Antonio, Christian, and Sebastian. Coincidently, almost a year into my marriage, my parents separated. From that moment on, my relationship with my father changed forever.

From being my friend, he disappeared from our lives for more than ten years initially, as we had long periods of disconnection and estrangement. He started a new family, and my resentment and lack of acceptance did not contribute anything to our rapprochement. Overnight, I felt that my father had been transformed into another person. I had grown up depending on his advice and approval, used to him helping me solve whatever problems I had in life. Suddenly, I felt lost, as if the floor had been taken away from me. I didn't know what to do, what to say, or where to go. My parents' relationship had not ended in the best of ways either. While it was true that this had been like a death foretold, my father leaving the house had taken us all by surprise.

The separation of my parents would be the beginning of a long learning process, in which I would have to begin to be independent and illuminate my path with my own light. This situation was exacerbated by my separation from Catherine and Antonio, our only child at the time, and by the loss of the last properties my parents owned. From one day to the next, I had been left without a family, without a home, and without money. I felt that everything was in chaos.

My mother was trying to deal with the sadness caused by the separation, while my brother, who was still living at home when my father left, was trying to understand what had happened. I, for one, had all kinds of questions in my head. In a way, this event had paralyzed our lives.

Because I had little understanding of spirituality, I did not know that this suffering would serve as an amplifier of learning for years to come. Today, I understand that this planet is a school where we come to learn through emotional experiences. Many of us get frustrated because we are looking for absolute happiness, but I think this can be very ephemeral. Those who are happy on Earth are those who enjoy learning, who take every test of life with positivity and encouragement to learn. I did not understand this concept at the time and that is why it caused me confusion and suffering.

Life still had several lessons and surprises in store for my mother, my brother, and me. Years later, we would understand the important role my father had played in our learning. A few days before his death - in June 2020 – while I was reviewing this book sitting on a chair next to the bed where he lay prostrate, I was able to put all the pieces of the puzzle together and close our circle of learning.

The months following my parents' separation and mine from Catherine, were very difficult. I had to face all kinds of circumstances, such as receiving room and board from my relatives. While this was a painful time, today I understand that this was only a contract between my father and me before I was reincarnated. I had to experience those shortcomings, the disconnection and separation, and then learn to forgive. I had to find myself, remember who I was and why I had come to this life.

Today I am aware that if my father had not almost disappeared from our lives all those years ago, I might not be who I am now, nor would I be doing what I am doing now. Everything happened as it was supposed to. I am the result of everything I had to live through, the good and the bad.

As I said before, one of the conditions we are exposed to when reincarnating on this planet is to go through a kind of spiritual amnesia. This, in fact, works to our benefit since we have experienced everything in past lives, whether considered good or bad in this dimension. We come here to learn by opposites, meaning that, generally, we begin to experience from childhood the opposite of what we will learn. If we come to learn about love, then we will first experience lovelessness. If we come to learn about self-love, then we must first experience low self-esteem and humiliation. To understand what day is, we must first experience what night is.

The great challenge we go through as incarnate spirits is to experience emotions. In spirituality, there is no such thing as good or bad, for everything is learning. My father and I chose that he would play this role in my reincarnation. Many will think this makes no sense at all. If spiritual contracts exist, why would I make this type of contract with my father's spirit? The answer is simple: for our spiritual evolution. We all seek to learn, experience, and help each other to continue to progress on this planet.

Spiritual awakening is the process by which we are reminded that we are spirits occupying a body. It is understanding that we are eternal spirits who go from reincarnation to reincarnation, learning and evolving, as part of a spirit group. Sometimes we come as parents and children, brothers and sisters, or spouses; we play the role of friend and enemy, victim and victimizer. Each of these roles has a specific purpose through which we will learn from love or suffering.

For my part, my relationship with my father was never the same after he left home when I was twenty-three. Although I was able to get closer to him on several occasions, it was always temporary and we ended up again with distance and resentment. It did not matter that I had already awakened spiritually -almost twenty years after he left home- nor did it matter that I already had a better understanding of why what had happened, had happened. My father continued to play the role he had agreed to play with me.

I admit that, for many years, I resented him and, above all, I was hurt. I did not want to expose myself and my family to that feeling again. I had already given up on restoring our relationship

My separation from Catherine lasted almost two years, during which I went through moments of loneliness, self-analysis, and planning. I had a lot of time to think about what had happened between the two of us. How was it possible that everything around me had collapsed so quickly? After this period of introspection, Catherine and I got back together and we had Christian and Sebastian, our children.

It was during that period of isolation that I met the first people who opened my eyes and mind to other realities, other dimensions. They were very humble and big-hearted people, willing to take the bread out of their mouths to share it with me, who saw me for who I really was and not for what I had or had had.

This was also the first stage - I realize that now when I look back - in which I felt the universe next to me, showing me its light. I am referring to the fact that it put very valuable people in my way, such as Miguel Sánchez "Lito," Edgar Cisneros "el moro" and Sonia, a family friend whom I consider an aunt. I will talk about them later when I refer to the points of support and encouragement that I found throughout my life

Suffering as an Amplifier of Learning

The history of humanity is full of sad and tragic events, both in individual experiences and in events that involved an entire town, country or race. Among the best known is the Jewish holocaust and the world wars, but there have also been earthquakes, tsunamis, and many other natural disasters that ended up sending the entire world into mourning.

Through each of these events, human beings have been able to raise their level of consciousness and understanding. We have learned the difference between what is right and what is wrong. These events have also allowed us to experience feelings of compassion for our neighbors located on the other side of the world, in a remote place that we do not even know about. Also, they brought us together and led us to help each other in the most difficult times.

How many times have we heard about personal tragedies through the media or social media - people with a terminal illness or who fell into disgrace for some reason - causing a group of individuals to come together to raise funds, to seek help, to alleviate their sorrows in one way or another. How many times have we witnessed the extraordinary response and result of that union and solidarity?

If we analyze each sad event, each tragedy or natural disaster, we will realize that, through suffering, we were able to learn lessons that we will never forget. Then, it would be logical to think that pain is an amplifier of learning. With each one of those experiences, the universe gives us the opportunity to experience and learn something new.

The truth is that nothing we experience is by chance, since each event was carefully planned by ourselves before we reincarnated. As I said before, my advice in these difficult circumstances is always to ask ourselves why it is happening to us and what we have to learn from it.

Today, when I look back in time, I realize that, in the saddest time of my life, I achieved greater learning through opposites. From having many comforts, I went from having almost nothing and receiving help from family members, from a plate of food to a word of encouragement. From growing up surrounded by love and family togetherness, I moved on to loneliness and heartbreak. From always feeling supported and protected, I went on to feel totally vulnerable and lost.

It wasn't until a year after my separation from Catherine that I made the decision to travel to the United States. I knew that the economic situation was not going to improve soon, and I had always felt that my future was outside of Peru.

On the other hand, I also thought that by putting distance between us, I would suffer less, but I could not have been more wrong. The United States was another school for me, as the life of an immigrant brings a whole new set of lessons; how it felt to be in a foreign place, to begin the ascent from the lowest step, to learn another language, customs and norms, and finally, to go through long working days in search of economic well-being.

Miami, Florida was the place I lived for many years before moving to Charlotte, North Carolina. That city is known for being full of immigrants of different nationalities. As I once heard someone say, every immigrant in Miami comes running away from something. It can be from a dictatorship, from civil wars, or from poverty. I was looking to escape from sadness, without knowing that it would follow me anywhere.

Those years were a time of much learning and work on myself. I learned to be humble by doing such dignified and basic jobs, such as washing dishes in a restaurant, to be patient while waiting for my mother's mail, where she would tell me how my brother and son were doing, to work as part of a team, and to push my body to the limit.

I also learned, through other immigrants, that each person is a world on its own, that each one has a story with joys and sorrows. Thanks to the stories of many Cuban friends, I understood what they had to go through to get to this country. Some came on a raft, others were petitioned by their parents, who had left when they were still very young. From every foreigner I worked with, I learned something. I was able to see their spirits without being influenced by their physical appearance. Those who were smiling, in fact, sometimes cried on the inside, and those who were crying, perhaps were happy to hear from their families. The school of the immigrant is one of suffering, but also of learning.

Many say that the United States changes you. I always heard stories from people who told how their families had been transformed by coming to this country. The truth is that America does not change you, but brings out your best strengths and your worst defects. In a way, Miami felt like a concrete jungle where everyone was doing what they had to do to survive, to bring bread to the table. I think the secret was always to let yourself be guided by your heart and not by your instincts, ego, or pride.

The following years were full of learning and introspection. I experienced joy, sadness, love, self-realization, and melancholy, among other deep emotions. Life as an immigrant was not easy and it helped me to value what I had in my country, my culture, and to be humble and grateful for the opportunities that were being given to me in a new land.

One of the feelings that I experienced during several of these years, was the resentment towards my father. Some time later, I understood that this was the role he should play in our lives. If my father had not left us, I would not have evolved and learned everything I learned from the very moment he left home. In a manner of speaking, and although it may not make sense to some, that grudge turned into gratitude and helped to heal my wounds little by little, as I walked the path of spirituality.

Healing Through Forgiveness

The human being is a repository of emotions, and many of these are trapped in our subconscious mind. Therefore, it is very common that we do not realize the consequences that they cause us. According to the mental model used by hypnosis practitioners to explain how the human mind works, the conscious part occupies 12% of our mind and the subconscious part occupies the remaining 88%. In our conscious part, there is reason and logic, the analytical part where our will power is found.

The mental model differs slightly from one school of thought of hypnosis to another, although all are similar. Anchored in a long tradition, modern neurology has largely confirmed these concepts. The tomography and the magnetic resonances endorsed by medicine reveal that brain activity seems to correspond very well to this mental model.

In the subconscious, we have positive and negative associations that we have created throughout our lives. For example, for the smoker, smoking may be associated with relaxation. For others, the action of eating could be associated with love. Perhaps food reminds them of their mother's love when she fed them as a child. And so, we can list multiple associations that we ourselves have created. Also in our subconscious, we can find traumatic events stored, which were encapsulated by the conscious mind and sent to the subconscious until the moment we are ready to deal with them.

Another way in which information is stored in our subconscious is through visualization and repetition. An example of this is in the martial arts, where the practitioners repeat countless times the attack and defense movements to such an extent that, after a while, these movements become instinctive. That is to say, when faced with a real attack, the body's reaction is instantaneous without even having to think or remember.

Another important component of our psyche is the critical mind, which divides the conscious and subconscious areas. It is the one that decides what is kept and what is not in the subconscious. It is the equivalent of the password that we have to enter to access the information on our computer.

The problem is that the critical mind is not fully developed when we are children. That's why most events are stored directly in the subconscious mind. Many of the emotional problems we have as adults originated during our childhood. And, since time does not exist for the subconscious mind, it makes us react the same way we did when that event took place, even though that reaction might not be according to our current age.

With no intention to confuse the reader, the same information that I have mentioned above is stored in our subconscious, but not only of our current life. Everything we have experienced in other reincarnations is also stored there.

That is why I have been able to meet clients who had unexplainable pains or phobias. Their bodies were completely healthy and they have never experienced any event in this life that has caused them such fear. When we do not deal with our repressed emotions stored in our subconscious, in time, they can manifest as physical symptoms, that is, in a psychosomatic way.

For example, Timothy J. Legg, a doctor who specialized in geriatric mental health and psychiatry, in an article published in the Healthline portal, confirms that repressed emotions can generate cancer, high blood pressure, migraines, and fibromyalgia, among other conditions. This does not mean that all people who experience illnesses do so because of repressed emotions, but that many of the illnesses we suffer from are also caused by our mind. That is, they are created by us.

If we stop to think, then healing these illnesses we created ourselves should not be so difficult. If we created them, we can also eliminate them. This could be achieved through personal work of introspection, but, above all, by the hand of forgiveness.

The Conscious Hypnosis Session

I had only been practicing the Introspective Hypnosis technique
for a short time when I received a call from Estela, who was interested
in scheduling a session with me. During my interview with her, and
as part of the process, she gave me a summary of her life, of those
more transcendental events and those that had marked her.

Estela suffered a lot during her childhood in Mexico, and then
during her first marriage to the father of her children. She told me in
detail about the traumatic events she experienced with her father and
other relatives, as well as everything she had to endure during her
marriage; from physical and emotional abuse, to having her children
taken away from her. At the time of the interview, they were already
teenagers and visited her from time to time.

We made a list of the issues she wanted to address in the session
and the expectations she had. The list contained about eight important items, which had in common their relationship with events that
caused her sadness, but above all, a lot of resentment. We began with
the induction process, in which I take my clients into a deep state of
relaxation similar to an altered state of consciousness.

I quickly noticed that Estela was in a very superficial trance.
When I asked her to travel through time in search of sad memories,
she found them without any problem and so we began to work on
them, even though I had the impression that she was just talking with
her eyes closed. During the rest of the session we visited the events of
her life related to the list of issues to work on. In each sad and traumatic event that Estela visited, we worked with forgiveness therapy.

I explained to her that not forgiving is equivalent to drinking a bottle of poison with the idea that she is hurting the other person when, in fact, she is hurting herself.

I explained that forgiveness is not about forgetting, not about making peace, not about stop seeking justice. It's making sure that that emotion doesn't hurt us, freeing us from those memories in our subconscious that have us trapped. When we finished the session, I told Estela that I wanted to see her again the next week, and that the second visit would be free of charge. I asked her to come back because I felt that she had not been able to work at subconscious level, which is usually the level where the biggest changes take place.

When Estela returned a week later, she had a different look on her face and seemed happier. I tried not to pay attention to that because I thought my optimism was influencing me, and that I was seeing things that might not really be true at all.

When we sat down to discuss her post-session experiences, I opened my notebook with the notes from our first meeting and we proceeded to review the list of issues to work on again. My goal was to find out if these were still the priority I had previously assigned them. When we began to review, item by item, Estela kept telling me that those symptoms had already disappeared; until we reached the last one. One of Estela's concerns was that, during her menstrual period, the bleeding had a very strong, unpleasant odor. When I asked her if she still wanted to work on it, she told me that the night before her period started, those characteristics were no longer there.

I was surprised. I had asked Estela to come back to work on unfinished business and there was none left. I then offered to work on her weight control - a problem she had told me about - since she was in my office and I didn't want her to feel like she had come for nothing. That day I learned two valuable lessons that would serve me in my practice of hypnosis and that I would carry with me for the rest of my life. First, for Introspective Hypnosis, no matter what level of trance our clients are in, everyone goes to the level they need to work on the session. And, second, forgiveness is one of the most important elements in the healing process of human beings.

By forgiving her ex-husband and others related to the most traumatic events in her life, Estela had freed herself from the repressed emotions she had kept for years in her subconscious mind. She had detached herself from those memories that held her back, creating an association according to the level of maturity and understanding of her age at the time. Estela now felt empowered, and had decided to take control of her life and the type of emotions that would be stored in her mind from that moment on.

The Abandonment of a Mother

Lourdes, a young woman in her early twenties, came to my office for a hypnosis session. She wanted to end the pain she was feeling all over her body, her sudden mood changes, and the intense headaches she was suffering from.

Lourdes was from South America. Her mother had abandoned her during her childhood when she decided to immigrate to the United States. She left her grandmother in charge, knowing that her little girl would not have a good time since she herself had suffered so much at her mother's hands. The grandmother's malicious behavior was in revenge for her husband - Lourdes' grandfather - from whom she separated when Lourdes was just a child.

Already in a deep hypnotic trance, Lourdes moved to the moment when her mother said goodbye to her and told her that she was going to leave her with her grandmother until she could take her with her. She relived that scene as if she were there, while I asked her questions so that she could see this event from another perspective and find the answers herself.

Her mother said goodbye and told her that she would not forget her, while Lourdes cried and asked her not to leave. This was an event that marked her deeply. At first, Lourdes refused to forgive her mother for leaving her, but when she saw that event from a spiritual perspective, she understood that the experience had made her stronger in her life. She understood the purpose of the event, instead of being stuck with the why. Also, she understood that she could not judge her mother because she had not received love from her and, therefore, did not understand how to give love.

Finally, Lourdes was able to forgive her mother and feel compassion for her. The session continued and she kept reliving other memories, among them, one in which she was abused by her stepmother as revenge on Lourdes' mother. After working through that event, she was also able to better understand what happened and forgive her.

Another sad moment that marked her very much was the death of her grandfather, who had passed away a few years ago. As one of the concepts of Introspective Hypnosis is that time does not exist, we started a conversation with her grandfather's spirit. He told me how much his granddaughter had suffered and gave me more details of what she had gone through. The grandfather also gave her several pieces of advice, among them, to forget everything that happened with her parents and grandmother. "Beautiful things await you in the future," he assured her. I remember that Lourdes' face lit up with joy when she heard his words. Grandpa had confirmed to her that forgiving and forgetting was the next step so that she could live in harmony and love, enjoying life with her husband.

By the end of the session, Lourdes remembered very little. She mentioned that she felt different and lighter, as if a weight had been lifted. A few months later, I called her and she told me that the pains had disappeared shortly after our meeting and that she was very happy about that. She had released the negative emotions she had been holding back. The understanding she gained allowed her to see those traumatic incidents from another perspective and to recognize the lesson behind them.

My Own Forgiveness

While it is true that my history and the events I have experienced are not as painful or complicated as those my clients bring to the sessions, I also went through a long process of forgiveness and understanding of my relationship with my parents.

Many might assume that this process was not so difficult for me because I was supposed to have a knowledge of spirituality already, but that is not entirely true. I was not always familiar with those concepts. While I believed in reincarnation, I did not have the understanding and experience that I gained many years later from my studies and sessions with my clients.

There were also times when I felt like a victim of fate, of an injustice. Moreover, I was so deluded that I believed that everything that happened to me was because of my father, for leaving home the way he did.

My healing process was long, painful, and slow, and was accompanied by all kinds of sad situations and negative emotions. Today when I look back, I understand that everything happened as it was supposed to, because it was the only way I could find myself, remember who I am, and discover my mission. In other words, you could say that I was in training. In order to help other people in the future to free themselves from repressed emotions and memories that held them back, I had to first learn how to free myself from all that.

Today I know that my father and I agreed that he would play that role in my life for my own good and evolution. If we start from the premise that we are part of a spiritual group in which we help each other evolve, we will understand that my father, out of love for us and surely at my request, decided to play that role.

It might sound logical to think that, if I had that understanding today, the relationship between us would have improved by almost one hundred percent, but that is not the reality. As long as we continue to sleep or choose to continue to sleep spiritually, we will continue to play the role we came to play in this reincarnation. In other words, we must understand that our life is a play tailored to our own spiritual evolution.

This is how, in every attempt I had to approach him, he kept playing the agreed upon role. This generated great pain in me after each failed attempt.

By the time I started writing this chapter, our relationship had improved tremendously. We were having a fluent dialogue and exchanging life experiences. When he was over seventy-six years old, he felt he had little time left, and we were able to work on forgiveness, each accepting our share of responsibility.

As I mentioned above, it was during the time I was reviewing what I had written in this book, over the course of a year and a half, that my father passed away. It was in June, 2020, two days after his seventy-seventh birthday. My father passed away, and so I was able to complete my learning cycle with him. I will give more details about this when I talk about forgiveness therapy.

Healing the wounds was not easy. It took many years and tears, but today, like the ancient warriors, I show my scars with pride because it means I was in battle and survived. Looking back, I can only have words of gratitude to the universe and to my father for every situation that I went through, whether it was pleasant or not. Each event brought out my worst defects, which I was able to work on to evolve with, but also my best virtues, which helped me remember who I was and what I came here for.

Throughout this process, I also learned from my mother, the unconditional and unexplainable love she had for my father, her optimism about life, her desire to fight, her spiritual strength, and her gift of service to others. If at any time I felt betrayed when I saw the love she still felt for my father, today I understand that we have all been together before. They chose to come to live their own experiences and learn from each other. For my part, I learned to respect that each spirit has its own process, its own agenda, its own lessons, and its own path to follow. The only thing left is to respect them, have compassion, and support them in their journey when they need it.

Today I know that, to do what I do, I needed to be raised by the best teachers, by those who put me through situations that would help me experience all kinds of emotions as I grew up. Today I understand that those teachers were my parents and for that I will live eternally grateful.

The Lessons in Common and Understanding of My Purpose

I do not consider my case special or too complicated, since I am aware that many have gone through even more complex moments than those I had to go through. However, it is precisely what happened to me that fitted the lessons I had to learn in order to fulfill my mission in life: to practice regressive hypnosis.

If there was one thing I realized at the beginning of my immersion in spirituality, it was that every person I met, like me, was learning regressive or spiritual hypnosis techniques. They had gone through practically the same process as I had. Each of them had been torn in half, so to speak, and had managed to heal themselves during their journey through this reincarnation. Now, they were ready to help others heal their wounds.

I could also perceive that the universe, the light, or their guides had developed their specialty in hypnosis and that, without realizing it, they were learning the techniques for that specialty to contribute to the healing of others.

In my case, I noticed that there was a common denominator in the type of client that came to me. They were usually people who had experienced not necessarily similar events to mine, but the same emotions. It was coincidentally that similarity that led me to empathize with my clients, since I myself knew what they were feeling.

It is the empathy, love, and intention with which we carry out our mission that allows our clients to have positive results after visiting us.

You could say that, since we were born, all the volunteers were in training to be able to fulfill our mission. Each one of us who planned to come and help with people's spiritual awakening, carefully planned each situation we would face when we reincarnated. I know that there are many other healing modalities and alternatives, but I can only speak of what I and my colleagues in the field of spiritual regressive hypnosis have experienced.

When I began teaching Introspective Hypnosis, a method based on that of my teacher, Aurelio Mejia, I was able to observe that the attendees, when visiting sad memories, had gone through very difficult events. They had all felt as if they were being torn in two, but at the same time, they had learned to heal themselves through love and forgiveness.

If there is one thing I have always felt, it was that I was looking for something that I could not define. At certain stages of my life, I could not find or identify with what I was doing. I was not content. Even the knowledge in computer systems that I obtained in the late nineties, when I specialized as a systems engineer specialized in computer networks, did not fill me up.

On the contrary, I was always attracted to metaphysics. All my life I felt a strong connection with service, helping, advising, and solving different situations for others, but I could not find something that would fill me up one hundred percent. It wasn't until I learned about regressive hypnosis and saw the transformation my clients were achieving, that I felt I had found what I had been looking for, for so long: my mission.

When I began conducting sessions, I saw how clients who came to me had been sent by the universe, for the path they were to walk was also marked by spirituality.

Conversation with a Grandmother Guide

During the initial interview, Claudia told me about the most important events of her life, starting with her childhood. She told me some sad anecdotes with her mother, as well as the lack of love that her mother had for her, and the molestation that she suffered at the hands of her father during her adolescence.

She had suffered a lot since she was little until her current marriage. Her life had been marked by deep sorrow, except for the time she lived with her grandmother, from whom she received only love.

Already in a hypnotic trance, she visited those sad and traumatic memories in order to work through them. Almost at the end of the session, I asked her to visualize her energetic body to verify that everything was white. I use this technique to detect if there are lost souls attached to my clients, since there are times when an attached spirit can be visualized as a shadow or a stain in our aura. To better understand this, I must point out that every person in trance is a potential medium, and many times they acquire extrasensory abilities.

Claudia told me that she was all white, but that she saw a light coming towards her. She described it as an intense purple light that landed on her chest. From the information provided in Michael Newton's book "Destiny of Souls" and the sessions with my clients, I knew that that purple energy could only be a more advanced spirit. I asked that energy to express itself through Claudia.

Antonio: Three, two, one. Brother, you can express yourself now, can you tell us who you are?

Spirit: I am her grandmother -she said in a soft voice-, I brought her to you.

A: Did you guide her to me? Do you know me?

S: Yes, I know you.

A: Can you tell me how you know me?

S: You are light.

A: And how did you find me, grandmother? Excuse me for asking, but I want to learn more about the spirit world. How did you find me?

S: You have an open channel that is only captured by higher spirits. That's how I found you.

A: Grandma, could you tell me what energies are with me?

S: You have yellow energy -she answered, referring only to me and not to the energies around me-. But you have to do things more out of love.

This was the first message I received from the spirit world, teaching me that we have to connect our hearts to those who come for help, so that we can facilitate the sessions with love.

S: You can get lost. You have to enter the purple light.

The communication with Grandma's spirit continued longer. She told me that her granddaughter had come to this reincarnation to go through all that she had gone through so that in her next reincarnation she could have a much more advanced energy. This was for her own evolution. Claudia had to see beyond her fears. The session ended after Grandma said goodbye, but before that she let her granddaughter know that she would always be with her.

This was the first time that a spirit confirmed and explained in detail that people are sent to therapists or regressive hypnosis practitioners by their guides, according to the tools, knowledge, or specialty that each of us has. In other words, no one comes to us by chance.

An Extraterrestrial on Earth

Shelia was interested in a Quantum Healing Hypnosis Technique session, which I learned directly from Dolores Cannon. It is based primarily on a regression to past lives by contacting the Higher Self or super consciousness, that part which is connected to the spiritual world and which stores all the information from this and other lives.

During the interview, Shelia mentioned to me that the main reason for the session was to find the cause and cure of a rash on her skin, a kind of rash that would constantly break out and cause her body to itch uncontrollably during the day, increasing at night to the point that it would not let her sleep.

I remember Shelia also told me about the projects she had with her husband, where they were trying out different methods of farming without using chemicals so as not to pollute the soil.

During the hypnotic trance induction, I noticed that she was quite nervous. I don't know if it was a fear of the unknown or because, on a subconscious level, she knew what was about to happen.

Once in a trance, I asked her to travel in time and space in search of a reincarnation where I could find information she needed for this one. I started by asking her to detail her body from head to toe. To her surprise, her description was not of human feet or limbs. When she began to list what she saw around her, it corresponded to a place on another planet with another type of terrain and environment. She indicated that she saw a kind of construction with something that resembled a door. I asked ger to go in and describe to me what she saw inside. Shelia told me that there were beings with the same kind of body as hers standing around a pond that contained a deep blue, water-like substance.

When the beings saw her, they invited her to join them. She was so frightened when she saw the scene that she opened her eyes and quickly came out of the trance. I tried to relax her and explain to her that it was important that she finish receiving that information, but in spite of trying to put her in a trance again, she was so nervous that she could not achieve it. After talking for a few moments, I asked her to come back in a week to try it again because I felt it was important to continue the meeting with those beings.

Almost a week later, the day before her appointment, Shelia called me to cancel her session because she was too busy. Deep down, I knew she wasn't ready to receive the information they had to give her. It wasn't until a month and a half later that she called me to ask if I could see her the following day. I agreed quickly.

Upon arriving at my office and after talking for a few minutes about what had happened in our previous session, we began the induction process to bring her into an altered state of consciousness again. This time, when I asked her to describe to me what she was observing, she told me that she was in some kind of theater or cinema, which she was invited to enter while being given a ticket.

When she entered the room, she detailed a place that had several seats and a large screen in front of it. Some people were sitting in the center looking at the screen when, suddenly, they turned to see her. She quickly realized they were the same beings who had tried to engage her in conversation in the previous session. They asked her to follow them, passed through a door, and led her into a beautiful garden surrounded by walls.

I knew that this time the beings had chosen to show themselves to her in a more relaxing environment so that she would not be frightened again by what was around her.

Once in the garden, they introduced themselves and let her know that she belonged to their race and planet. They reminded her that she had volunteered to reincarnate on Earth to learn and accumulate experiences to take back to her planet after this life.

This time, Shelia was more relaxed and in a deeper trance. I didn't have to do much for her to get the information she needed, just ask her to repeat everything she was being told so that it would be recorded. I also advised her not to analyze what she was being told, as she would have time for that later.

The conversation between Shelia and the visitors continued for almost 45 minutes, during which I became a mere spectator. They shared a lot of data, concepts, formulas, images, diagrams, and techniques to achieve the crops she wanted, and the place where she should buy that land. I could tell that she was fascinated by the information she received. I, of course, was as amazed as she was.

When the beings completed the transmission of that information, I asked permission to ask them a few questions that Shelia had brought to the session. They agreed without hesitation. I told them that one of the main reasons why she came to see me was the rash he suffered on her body and the uncontrollable itching it caused. They replied that if she hadn't had that skin problem, she simply wouldn't have come looking for me. That is, they had created that symptom so that she would look for me, make an appointment, and in the midst of the hypnotic trance, receive everything she needed for her mission on Earth.

Antonio: So now that she's received the message, she doesn't need the rash -I asked in amazement.

Beings: No, not anymore.

A: Then, can it be removed?

B: Yes -they answered with complete certainty-. We already removed it.

When Shelia came out of the trance, we were both surprised by everything that had happened. I was speechless about the amount of information they had shared with her during the time of communication. She on the other hand, was perplexed to learn that she belonged to their race, and that she had come to this planet for a specific reason.

After talking for a few more minutes, Shelia said goodbye and left. It wasn't until almost a week later that I received a text from her on my cell phone with a picture showing me her arm with a red rash. At first, I thought she was sending me the photo to tell me she still had the same problem, but then she wrote:

Antonio, that's how my arms and my whole body used to be, causing me an uncontrollable itch all day and especially at night, without letting me sleep. After the session, I only felt an itch the next day, but since then it disappeared completely. I wanted to wait a few days to confirm that it wasn't my imagination and that the beings had taken that discomfort away from me.

This message fully validated what Shelia had experienced while in a trance. It also confirmed the veracity of the communication she had had with the alien creatures and the answers she got to several of the questions I asked them. With this session, I had understood that, using this type of hypnosis techniques, I was also at the service of other beings who needed to communicate with their group members incarnated on this planet.

I remember, that day I felt a great gratitude to the universe for the role I came to play in this life, for having the honor of serving as a bridge of communication for beings from other civilizations, and advanced spirits whose role was to guide. What I did not suspect at the time was that this was just the beginning, a sample of what would come for me in the future and what I would have to do and witness.

In the years that followed, I would realize how each past and future situation had been carefully orchestrated before my birth. This information would come to me through psychics, spirits that would manifest during my sessions, spiritual guides for my clients and, most importantly, what I would gain from my own search, my remembering, and my tying up of my introspection process. I will talk about this later.

I never imagined how much I would heal through the sessions with my clients, listening to the events in their lives during the initial interview, the information received during their session, and the messages that would be sent to me from the spirit world through them. I can safely say that the person I was when I started my journey through the field of regressive hypnosis, is not the same person who writes this book today almost seven years later.

Feeling Lost

All of us, at some point, have felt confused and aimless. It is during these periods that we find it difficult to make decisions and changes in our lives, as it becomes difficult for us to see beyond our noses. How many times have we seen a loved one in that situation not knowing what to do? For those of us who see that situation from the outside, the solution seems very simple and obvious, but the other person doesn't see it, and, some might decide not to listen to others.

While it is true that I have experienced those moments on multiple occasions, I think there were two events that marked me deeply and that took place very close to each other. As I have mentioned before, I refer to the separation of my parents and my wife Catherine along with Tony, my only child at the time. It was there that I felt as if the floor that kept me standing had been taken away from me. I just didn't know what to do or where to go.

For a while, I was in a kind of vegetative state and suspended in time and space. They say that one of the factors affecting our mood is the thing we focus on during that period. It is not difficult to figure what my mood was during that time, as my mind and heart were focused on the great sadness I felt and trying to make sense of the great upheavals that had taken place in my life and my family's. It seemed as if I was living a nightmare.

Usually, all spiritual evolution and transformation begins with a great sense of discomfort. When I talk to my clients, I give them the example of the hermit crab and its growth process. The shell of this crab never grows. So how does the animal get to the size it will have as an adult? While it is true that the shell does not grow, what does grow is the crab inside the shell. When it feels uncomfortable and tight, it leaves its shell and begins to look for a new one. This process is repeated several times until the crab reaches its adult size. If we think about what motivates the crab to keep growing, we can easily deduce that it is the feeling of discomfort and tightness. These sensations push it to leave the old shell to find a new one.

In the same way, the greatest evolution and spiritual growth in our lives occurs when we are stimulated by the feeling of discomfort, uncertainty and being lost. At the end of the day, it is up to us how we choose to face those moments, whether or not we know how to make the most of them. As I said before, the key is not to ask why we are going through this, but what do we have to learn. Financial problems, divorces, infidelity of the spouse, the death of a loved one, and the feeling of abandonment, among other circumstances, are what affect us psychologically and emotionally.

All these events, in fact, will allow us to evolve through love and forgiveness, as long as we are open to it. As I have mentioned before, something I have learned through the hypnosis sessions I have facilitated in the last few years, is that we plan our reincarnation ourselves. We carefully choose all the good and bad situations - although, in the spirit world, there are no negative experiences since everything is learned - that we will go through. We plan a series of circumstances that will allow us to evolve spiritually when we reincarnate.

We have already spoken of the amnesia to which we are subjected upon coming to planet Earth, but there is also the illusion of separation or individuality, when in reality we are all one. Not only do we face the challenge of remembering who we really are, but also of how to deal with the situation we are facing. It is very common for human beings to choose not to take responsibility for what is happening, and therefore have difficulty visualizing the opportunity for learning and change that is presented to them. Some will choose to feel like victims of fate or of others, a few will choose to blame others for what they have experienced, while others will simply do nothing, preferring to close their eyes and accept what happened without feeling anything about it.

When I had to live what I mentioned above, I did not yet have the knowledge of spirituality and reincarnation that I have now. Although I describe it as a temporary vegetative state, I remember that, trying to make sense of everything that had happened, I started a stage of introspection, in which I looked for what I could have done wrong and what I should change. Without going into too much detail so as not to bore anyone, it would basically be these facts that would lead me to that state of discomfort and in turn, to the search for myself.

Like the process of growth of the hermit crab, this would be the beginning of events that I would face throughout my life to help me in my spiritual evolution.

THE POINTS OF SUPPORT AND
THE EXTREME EXPERIENCES

In different parts of this book, I have talked about how we plan our reincarnation. We all choose our birthplace, our parents and every lesson or test we will go through, and we make contracts with other spirits who will play specific roles in our lives - whether in pleasant or unpleasant situations - that we will encounter once we are reincarnated.

Within that careful planning, there is also the choice of the body that will best lend itself to achieving our goals for the next life. For example, those who feel the need to experience limitations may choose bodies with disabilities, and those who need to experience discrimination will choose to be of a specific race, religion, or sexual orientation. Michael Newton wrote in detail about this topic in "The Destiny of Souls," and I have been able to corroborate this during my sessions.

We have free will both in the spirit world during the planning stage, and once we arrive on Earth. This means that when we are presented with a test, it is entirely up to us how to live it and what option and action to take.

Some will think that there is no point in planning a lesson to learn something specific when there is a possibility that, due to the spiritual amnesia and illusion of separation that we experience when reincarnating, we will stray from our path and not obtain the learning and spiritual evolution of the event. The truth is that lesson planning is a little more complex than one might think. Let's remember those school or university exams where there were multiple options as an answer, that is, when a question is followed by four or more possible answers, from which we must select the correct one. Now, let's imagine that there is no wrong answer and that any answer has a certain degree of correctness. This is exactly how the spiritual world works. There is no such thing as right or wrong, for in the end, everything is about learning.

Going back to the example of the multiple-choice test where it doesn't matter which answer is chosen, let's think about some complicated circumstance that we've had to live through. Then, let's imagine all the possible options, paths, or alternatives that that situation offered. Let's analyze the consequences or effects that each one of those alternatives would have had if we had chosen them. Now, let's try to imagine what we would have learned from each of those choices, and we will realize that in the end, there would always have been a learning curve. Those teachings could have been acquired in a context of love or suffering, but, in the end, the learning always took place.

Each lesson provides different options that we can choose, and each one provides different learning, but we must consider that we are never alone. We have our spirit guide or guardian angel assisting us whenever we ask.

Spirit guides are advanced spirits whose function is to guide, as their name indicates. They are with us in the most difficult and darkest moments to give us a hand. It is these beings of light who constantly assist us so that we do not deviate from the path we have laid out. Many times, they prevent us from certain events and dangerous places. They communicate with us through thoughts they place in our minds. André Luiz's spirit, channeled by the medium Chico Xavier, gave them the name of magnetic passes in the books "Missionaries of Light" and "Spiritual Messengers".

The truth is that, when our body needs to regain energy during our sleep, our soul does not stay inside of it waiting for it to wake up. The soul leaves the body to perform other activities. It is in this state that beings of light, including our deceased loved ones, communicate with us for different reasons. Once we wake up, we remember it as a very vivid dream, when in fact it was not.

This telepathic or magnetic communication can also be had with people around us and thus receive the message through them.

The spirit world, as described by André Luiz's spirit, has several relief groups at different levels, both on our physical plane, in the area called "purgatorial," and in the spiritual community, which will be our final destination.

We are never alone. We have the necessary assistance, as long as we are the ones who ask for it. The beings of light and spiritual guides will respect our free will at all times.

How many times have we heard of stories where someone who was about to board a plane that ended up crashing, decided to change his flight or simply missed it at the last moment? These are our spiritual guides in action.

Just like a trainer or a fitness coach, the guides continually help us move forward. They remind us of what we came here to do, and many times they send us messages through other people. Hasn't it ever happened to you that a stranger came up to you and gave you just the answer to a question you were asking yourself?

The universe uses different methods to make sure that our plan follows its course and is carried out according to what we have planned.

Accidents and Near-Death Experiences

"Your Soul's Plan," by Robert Schwartz, with whom I had the honor of communicating on a couple of occasions, and from whom I received the book directly, explains in detail the process of pre-birth planning. His book lists several cases of people who faced complicated events, such as the loss of a loved one, addiction, a delicate illness, and serious accidents. This information was obtained through mediums or channels -as they are called now- who communicated with their own guides to explain the reasoning behind why each of these people had to go through it.

In a way, what Robert found through his years of research can be compared with the information that other professionals, such as Brian Weiss, Michael Newton, and Dolores Cannon, found during the thousands of hypnosis sessions with their clients or patients. Later, following the teachings of my teachers, I obtained the same results in my own sessions. My clients were able to go to the moment of planning in the spiritual world, and they themselves related why they had chosen this or that lesson.

As a contingency plan and to ensure learning, we sometimes choose events that will radically change our lives. These have the particularity of achieving a rapid awakening of consciousness to lead us to take an action plan or retake it. Such events could be planned accidents, although, by the very fact of being planned, they should not be called accidents.

Cecile's Clinical Death

Some accidents or eventualities are so strong that they can lead us to die clinically for a few minutes. That was the case of Cecile, who died for a few minutes while giving birth to her daughter, as a consequence of a reaction to the anesthesia.

It was never Cecile's intention to have a hypnosis session. She never made an appointment with me, nor did she plan to do so. Cecile came to my office to pick up her mother, who had just had an Introspective Hypnosis session with me.

While Cecile was waiting in the car, I decided to accompany her mother to the car while saying goodbye and thanking her for bringing her mom. Cecile lived four hours away from Charlotte, North Carolina, where I live, and had taken the day off work to bring her mother.

When I approached the driver's window, Cecile smiled at me nicely and we introduced ourselves. She told me that she was considering coming in for her own session someday, not suspecting that the universe had used her mother to bring her to my office to receive a message.

I realized that I was dealing with a very interesting case. Something inside me made me ask her to come into my office for a few minutes to do some suggestibility tests, and determine how easily she went into a trance, so I could determine if she should come back later. The truth is that I knew that, if she initiated the trance without any problem, I would facilitate the session immediately and at no cost so as not to miss the opportunity.

Once in my office, Cecile took a seat and I began to perform some suggestibility tests. She went into a deep trance very quickly while her mother observed everything. When I asked her to look for a sad memory while I counted from five to one, she went to the day her daughter was going to be born. She described the scene from the moment she started getting her things ready to go to the hospital. She was with her husband and felt super happy.

When I asked her to go ahead to the next event, she moved to the moment when she was in the clinic bed wearing a white gown. Until that moment, she said she felt fine, but then her doctor arrived to examine her and Cecile informed her that she could not breathe. She said her heart was beating very fast and she felt as if she was asphyxiating. The situation continued to worsen until she heard the doctor ask to open an operating room to begin the C-section, indicating that the fetus was not well. When I asked her once again to move forward with the experience, she simply fell silent.

This is when I asked her if he had already closed her eyes and stopped breathing. To help her, I told her that she could get out of her body to see everything from above and she immediately started to describe the scene to me from that perspective. Her body was on the bed. She was able to watch them take her out of the room to the operating room and, with tears in her eyes, told me that the doctor was worried because she was not responding.

Cecile indicated that she saw many people around her, including her husband, who remained very worried in the room. On a spiritual level, I asked her a few questions.

> **Antonio**: While you are on that plane, outside your body, see if someone comes for you or if you go somewhere. What do you perceive while you are outside your body?
>
> **Cecile**: I seem to hear someone.
>
> **A**: What is she saying to you?
>
> **C**: Cecile, it's not your time yet.
>
> **A**: Where is that voice coming from?
>
> **C**: I just hear it. It's from a woman.
>
> **A**: Describe this woman to me. You can see with your spiritual eyes. How does it look?
>
> **C**: She has a beautiful face. She is neither young nor old.
>
> **A**: Does she have any clothes?
>
> **C**: No, she has something loose.
>
> **A**: Does it have energy?
>
> **C**: Yes, very pretty, clear.

A: Using telepathy, ask her who she is and tell me what she says.

C: An angel! -she said in surprise.

A: Do you know if that angel is the one assigned to you?

C: Yes.

A: Can you ask your angel what her name is?

C: Anna, she says -she answered immediately.

At that point, I asked her to ask Anna if we had permission to ask her some questions. She said yes. I asked Cecile to lend her mind and her lips so that I could talk to her.

Antonio Sangio: Ana, thank you very much for the communication. Are you Cecile's spirit guide?

Ana: Yes, she answered in a very soft voice.

AS: Ana, what is happening with Cecile? Why does she have to go through that experience?

A: I want her to have faith.

AS: Could you tell us faith in what or who?

A: Faith in God.

AS: She hasn't had faith so far?

A: Yes.

AS: Then why does she need this proof?

A: Because things have happened to her that have made her doubt.

AS: Does she know what you are talking about?

A: Yes -she answered as tears streamed from Cecile's eyes.

AS: What do you want to tell her?

A: That God will always take care of her and guide her.

AS: Those tears coming from Cecile's eyes, what are they about?

A: Of suffering.

AS: And why did she choose this suffering for this life? Is she allowed to know what she came to learn?

A: Forgiveness

The session continued for several more minutes. Cecile's mother was surprised to see what was happening in front of her eyes. When I thought I had enough information, I asked Cecile to focus again on what was happening to her body down there. She told me that she was seeing a lot of movement. After a few seconds, I directed her to return to her body and that is when she told me that her body began to awaken.

Ana, Cecile's spiritual guide, used the near-death event to give her a break so she could receive the message loud and clear: "you must have faith and you must learn to forgive".

Since this was not a planned session, I had not been able to have the initial interview with her and therefore did not know exactly what had happened in her life. What was important was the advice she had received while she was clinically dead.

Cecile did not remember everything that had happened while her body was dead. For her, all those details she gave while she was out of her body were a surprise. While it is true that on a spiritual level, she had already received the message: the universe never leaves loose ends. That is why it conspired to have her come and pick up her mother so she could experience a hypnosis session to remember her angel's advice.

If she was to remember that message on a conscious level, I can infer that she had not yet made that change in her behavior. In other words, by that time, the lesson of faith and forgiveness had not yet been fully learned.

Clinical Death in Another Life

Another case that can provide us with information about near-death experiences is that of Amanda, who came to my office to work on some emotional blocks.

In those days, I was still in the middle of training to obtain my certification as a therapist in the Life Between Lives technique, created by Michael Newton, author of the book. "Destiny of Souls." Since I knew that Amanda was one of those people who would go into a deep trance, I thought she would be an excellent candidate for this type of session.

Almost two months after our first session, Amanda returned, eager to gain more knowledge. We began with the typical induction and regression in time to her childhood memories, and then moved on to those in her mother's womb. Amanda had no trouble describing each stage in detail.

Then we continued to go back in time to the most recent or significant past reincarnation. In that life, she was a woman of African descent who lived without much trouble. First, we visited the event of her daughter's birth at age twenty-five. She was happy, even though the child's father was not present. She told me that she was used to it because of the job he had.

When I asked her to move forward to another important event in that reincarnation, she arrived to a scene where she was in the kitchen and suddenly began to feel a very sharp pain in her belly to the point that she fell to the floor. After spending a few minutes on the floor, she began to describe to me how she was coming out of her body. This made me think that this was the moment she was dying.

As soon as her spirit left her body, she expressed great sadness because she believed she had achieved nothing significant in that reincarnation. She felt she could have done more, but had simply preferred to remain in her comfortable role as a housewife, leaving everything else aside.

After a few minutes of floating above her body, I asked her to make her way home to the spirit world. Amanda - Didi in that life - began to feel herself rising as she saw an intense white light in front of her. I asked her to continue to ascend, but she said she felt she could not go any further. She expressed the feeling that there was something pulling her down, and that someone was telling her it wasn't her time yet.

Didi descended into her body and rejoined it. It had only been a near-death experience.

Antonio: Why did you have to go through that experience?

Didi: It's a lesson.

A: What did you have to learn?

D: To do what I was supposed to do.

A: And what were you supposed to do, Didi?

D: I wasn't doing anything.

A: Nothing that you had planned before you were reincarnated?

D: That's right.

In this case, there was no connection to a spirit guide for further information. But in reality, when we are in a trance and in a state of super consciousness, that is, in the consciousness that we have when we are out of the body, we have access to all the knowledge that we need. The limiting experience of being in a physical body in such a dense dimension along with an illusion of separation does not exist in that state. And that is where the messages are given to us by other beings of light or directly from the source.

As she continued to navigate through that life as Didi, Amanda described waking up in a hospital. The cause of the pain was the loss of the child she was carrying. As we moved forward in time, she told me that she now had a new purpose. From that near-death event to her death in that life, she had dedicated herself to helping people by giving clothing and food to those who needed it most. Didi's life ended up leaving her with a great sense of satisfaction for what she had been able to accomplish.

I know that many will wonder why Amanda needed to visit that past life. What is the point of visiting something that has already happened and in a favorable way? What information should she get from it?

One thing I have learned in my journey through the field of hypnosis is that when someone goes into a past life, it is because there is something to be gained or understood from what they experienced. Almost one hundred percent of the time what you receive from that reincarnation is related to situations you are going through now. In Amanda's case, she was going through a similar circumstance, where she was forgetting what she had come to do in this life.

In the current reincarnation, Amanda had always kept herself busy studying and obtaining professional degrees and certifications. While she was fulfilling her role as a mother and wife, she did not want to be a full-time housewife. This was related to what she had experienced as a Didi. Once again, Amanda was ignoring her mission.

When we discussed Didi's past life with her spiritual guide, whom we communicated with later in the session, the message was that she should help others, just as Didi did.

The Support Points

There are times when, from the spirit world, we make agreements with other spirits to help us avoid deviating from our path as part of our learning, or simply people and situations are put in our path by our spirit guides to help us at certain times. These are the typical people who appear "out of nowhere" and push us to take the path again, to get to the next level or to make the decision that will most favor our future. As we evolve, this happens several times. To talk about these people, I will refer to them as points of support.

I remember that, in the saddest or densest moments of my life, in those moments when I felt lost, disoriented and aimless, three points of support appeared on the scene. These three people, without even knowing it, played a specific and important role in my life, especially for the direction I would take many years later: helping others find their way through regressive and spiritual hypnosis sessions.

Each one of them, in their own way and with the knowledge and tools they had, knew how to give me the push and encouragement to continue seeing life from another perspective, that of spirituality. Thanks to their guidance, I was able to keep the course the universe had set for me at a time when any bad decision would have changed the story you are reading in this book.

My Aunt Sonia

Sonia, aunt as I call her, is a good friend of my maternal family. Her sister is the wife of my mother's cousin and that's how she had known me since I was little. Although I only saw her at a few family gatherings during my childhood and adolescence, it was easy for me to establish a trusting relationship with her. There was something about Sonia that inspired me with that confidence. I didn't know many details about her life, but I did know that she was very good at reading the tarot.

In 1992, almost shortly after my parents separated, my brother's girlfriend decided to break off their engagement. A few months later, it would be my turn to go through the separation from my wife, Catherine. That's how strange our lives were developing within the family. In a short time, my family had become chaos, and each of us was saddened to have to deal with this situation. But how could it be possible that my mother, my brother, and I were experiencing the same thing simultaneously?

At the time, I couldn't make any sense of what was happening, so I decided to turn to Sonia for guidance. I had never experienced a tarot reading and didn't know what to expect from her. I was both nervous and doubtful, as many people believed that the spirits had to be used to read the cards. Today I see it as a series of symbols and archetypes through which our Higher Self gives us information that we all have access to since, in the long run, we are all one and we are all connected.

The amount of data and the number of messages Sonia gave me that day was really impressive. I didn't understand how it was possible for one person to get so much information about my life, about things I hadn't told anyone. She informed me of some kind of work - witchcraft or psychic attack - that had been carried out against our family.

I didn't know what to think about it, but if she had been right about everything else she had told me, why wouldn't she be right about this too? Sonia recommended that I ask for the help of a shaman or healer to do a cleanse. I had nothing to lose. She didn't know any of them, but a client of hers had given her good references for one in particular, Edgar Cisneros or "el moro", as his friends called him.

Over the next few months, Aunt Sonia continued to help me through the tarot readings. These served me as a kind of compass or GPS while I navigated through those sad and uncertain times. Even though today I was not used to finding out what the future holds for me, everything Sonia said that the future held for me came true, including going to live in the United States and other events that happened years later.

Although it is true that Sonia helped me a lot with her guidance through the readings, what I still appreciate most was that I was able to count on a friendly voice. She gave me a lot of life advice based on her own experience and that of her clients. Without going into too much detail, she also gave me a preview of what was to come for me many years later. Although she did not know how to explain what she saw in her cards, she always told me that Catherine and I would be together again later on, and that I would travel a lot because of my work. Some time later, I resumed my relationship with my wife, and the trips she spoke of were fulfilled beginning in 2019, when I started practicing and teaching hypnosis full time. My first reading with Sonia took place in 1992.

Miguel Sanchez "Lito"

Another person who played an important role in that dark period of my life was Lito, of whom I spoke near the beginning of this book. He had been a friend of my mother's brother since they were young, and they had maintained their friendship over the years, contacting each other occasionally. The only thing I remembered hearing from Lito were my parents' comments about his knowledge of metaphysics and the reading of the Egyptian tarot. When my relatives found out about the situation I was going through, they recommended that I pay him a visit. Thus, I contacted him to make an appointment.

That was the first time I saw him. When I arrived at his house and he opened the door, I felt peace in his eyes and the energy in his house was just as peaceful. Lito introduced me to his wife, Raquel, and the three of us talked for a few minutes. Once in his office, he told me that he had been waiting for me, that he knew that I would be looking for him. He told me that my father had recently visited him and that he was more or less aware of the situation.

Lito, who was almost the same age as my father, started giving me life advice based on his own experience. It was as if he was giving me a complete x-ray of my problem and proposing very logical actions, but in the phase I was in, I could not see beyond my nose. At that moment, I could not see things from his perspective.

His tarot readings were different. They were not trying to predict my future, but to help me understand what I was going through. You could say that it was a therapeutic reading to invite reflection and corrective action on my behavior.

Lito began to place the cards on his desk and, while he did so, I focused on the bright colors and different symbols that each one of them had. As he positioned them, he told me what each one represented. One symbolized the mind, another the heart, and the others sexuality; what was happening to me and how I was going to handle it, and what we will face in the future and how I was going to handle it.

When he took out the last card of that throw, he told me that it spoke of my personality, of who I was. After a few seconds of silence, he stated that that card represented the son of God. I remember, with a smile on my face, I replied that there was nothing special about that card because we are all really God's children. He looked at me smiling and said, "Yes, that's right. But what this card tells me is that you have come for something special." I still didn't understand and he tried to explain to me better: "In a play, there are main actors, secondary actors and there are others who are only part of the set. In this life, you have been given a main role, there is something you must do."

That was the first time anyone talked to me about a special mission. Those words stayed in my mind for many years as I tried to understand what he meant. It wasn't until almost twenty-five years later that I understood what Lito had told me that day in 1992. I would later discover that the mission he was talking about was the practice of regressive and spiritual hypnosis, where I would not only help my clients, but also help lost souls find the light. The reading continued for several more minutes and the advice I received from Lito was invaluable.

On another of my visits, I asked him if he could teach me to read the tarot as he did. He kindly agreed, but made it clear that he would only give me part of the knowledge because the rest I would have to get for myself through time and my own research.

In a short time, I learned to read the tarot, which helped me to develop my extra-sensory perception and to be more compassionate. For the first time, I experienced receiving people who were desperate for help and guidance, but also many who only wanted to look into their future, ask frivolous questions, and achieve change without any effort. Soon after, I felt that this was not my thing and I did not continue to facilitate readings. In just a few months, the tarot had served its purpose.

With my move to the United States at a time when neither the Internet nor e-mails existed, I was losing track of Lito. It wasn't until mid-2018 that I was able to establish contact with him again through social media. I told him everything that had happened in my life and what I was doing now. I was able to thank him for everything he had done for me without charging a single penny and told him that I had finally understood what he had told me in my first reading about my mission. Lito was very happy to hear this. He is still helping and guiding others through his group.

Edgar Cisneros "el moro"

Once Aunt Sonia contacted her client, who had told her about an excellent healer, she received the contact number. Edgar lived in the city of Pisco, south of Peru's capital, but traveled to Lima on Saturdays to see to his clients during a shamanic session called *"mesa"*. The table is a kind of magic altar used by Peruvian shamans with the intention of healing and helping.

Despite its name, this is not really a table, but rather uses the soil - the earth or the *pachamama* - to have a better connection with nature. The table consists of several elements, such as the arts -carved wooden sticks-, the lagoons -bottles with liquids and different herbs- huacos -ceramic pieces produced by pre-Hispanic Peruvian cultures coming from the Andes- and swords. Each object has a specific function in the session.

The day I met Edgar, or the master, as his clients called him, was at Mrs. Estela's house, who lent it out for these meetings. The table started at midnight, but the attendees arrived from various parts of the city after eight o'clock and waited patiently. The session could hold up to twenty people and, depending on the number of people present, it could last until five in the morning.

I remember the first time I arrived around nine o'clock at night, there were already several people sitting on benches placed on both sides of the room. The table or altar was against one of the walls, forming a kind of U shape with the seats.

Edgar (Moro), a short man with brown skin, arrived almost at midnight. After greeting everyone, he asked us to form a line to drink "the medicine," a concoction obtained after boiling several herbs together with San Pedro, an original cactus from South America with a great Andean medicinal tradition. The natives consider this substance to be a spirit-opener. The session began with music, chants and dances by the participants, and then everyone took their seats. Lights were turned off and suddenly the room was illuminated only by the light coming through the window facing the street.

Edgar called each of us one by one. He asked us to stand in front of him, while he was sitting on the bench against the wall, but in front of the table. He asked us to say our name, turn around and walk to the other end of the room. The light coming in from the street meant that only the silhouette of the person could be seen, forming a kind of shadow.

As the individuals walked closer or further from the table, "Moro" would make his chungana - maraca or rattle - sound, while whistling and interpreting chants from the northern healers. Every so often, he would ask us to stop and walk again, going from the table to the window a couple of times while he tracked us. This is what they call the use of his psychic vision to determine what is happening to the person. Without having any information about us, he would tell us what was wrong with us or what problem we were having. The assistants would confirm what he was telling them. It was unbelievable.

Moro used everything that happened around him to track the person. If a dog barked outside, it meant arguments or fights, the vision of a condor could be interpreted as the death of someone close by, the crowing of a rooster represented triumph. As he tracked us, he asked others to give him certain "arts": carved canes. The eagle, for example, allowed him to have a remote vision of a specific place. King Solomon would help him enunciate words of wisdom to the seeker. The whistling huacos were used to clean and illuminate the energy. The swords were used to cleanse bad energies. Each element had a specific function.

When it was finally my turn to stand in front of the table and in front of him, he asked me to say my name and to start walking so he could track me. Immediately, he began to tell me everything that was happening in my life at that time, even talking about things that no one knew. Much of his advice coincided with what Aunt Sonia had also told me. Using the eagle for his remote vision, he described to me the apartment of my in-laws, the distribution of the furniture, the rooms, and even told me that it was a high place because, through the window, you could see the treetops, which was totally true.

My session was over in a few minutes and Moro asked me to come back and see him twice more. I was more than surprised. That day my mind opened to another world, to another dimension that would take me years to understand. How was it possible for a man who knew nothing about me, to describe in detail the apartment where my wife, Catherine, and my son, Tony, lived? How could he visualize people and describe their physical appearance and emotions? I knew there were many charlatans scamming people by posing as healers, but in Edgar I had found a true and well-intentioned shaman.

The other people who attended also showed surprise and admiration for what they had been told. Others had attended on other occasions and commented on how accurate and good he was. On my next two visits I experienced more of the same. I was constantly surprised by what he did and said. Today I see those elements I used as an aid to working on the energetic body and raising the frequency of our vibration as energetic hygiene.

After my third visit, Edgar asked me if I would like to continue attending his shamanic sessions at no cost. At that time, I was separated from Catherine and was in a very bad financial condition. I accepted, and decided to visit him from time to time and witness what he and his assistants were doing while helping his clients.

The truth is that, for a little over seven months, I attended almost religiously to all of his sessions. We became good friends and used to talk about different aspects of curanderismo (shamanism) and metaphysics. I remember that I was looking forward to Saturday to meet with those I already considered my friends. The owners of the house invited me to arrive earlier than the others so that we could talk more quietly.

It was during this period that I considered dark in my life that I met people of modest condition, but with a great heart and wisdom, open to sharing with me their food, their home, and their family. I have not forgotten them and I always carry them in my heart. During the months that I frequented Moro, my mind became more and more open. I understood that each person is a world and that we all have difficult moments. I learned to see people as spirits occupying temporary physical bodies and not to judge others by their physical appearance or economic status.

I witnessed the suffering of parents for the loss of their children, for the abandonment of a loved one, for drug addiction. I was exposed to a world that I did not know, from which my parents had protected me. I felt as if I had been in a bubble isolated from all suffering. I was getting to know the world as it is, but more importantly, I was learning to have compassion and empathy for others. Without realizing it, the seed of the spiritual volunteer began to germinate in me little by little.

Over the months, I even began to assist Edgar in his sessions with his cousins. The sessions were almost over at dawn, and although I was tired, I still felt a sense of satisfaction. After a little over seven months, in 1993, I made the decision to move to the United

States. Keeping in touch with Edgar and the others in the group became more difficult to the point of losing track. It wasn't until after the creation of social media that we got in touch again, a few years before writing this book.

Despite my telling him repeatedly, Edgar still fails to understand the role he played in my spiritual journey. But what we both do know is the friendship and respect we have for each other.

THE TEACHERS

The universe, our guides, and the very planning of our reincarnation, ensure at all times that our free will does not take us away from the plan that has been laid out. As I mentioned before, accidents, near-death experiences, and footholds serve as instruments to keep our course. But there are also other types of events that can generate a strong turn in our lives, motivating us to make radical changes.

If throughout this book I have shared with you what my mission is, it is not only because I feel it, I deduce it, or because of what I have read about, but also because of the messages that have been transmitted to me by beings of light through my clients in trance. The most logical thing would be to assume that, on my way, I should meet people who would fulfill the role of teachers in my life, like Sonia, Lito and Edgar, who guided me each in their individual ways and with their knowledge. However, now I want to refer to teachers who taught me the techniques that I will use for the rest of my life as I carry out my mission.

I emphasize again that I do not consider myself someone special or with an important role that puts me above others. I believe that I am just one volunteer like there are thousands in the world, fulfilling different functions and using different techniques and modalities. As I said before, my first months in the United States were not easy, as is the case with many immigrants in this country. Although it is true that with the passing of time, I was able to graduate as a systems engineer and work in the computer field for many years and with great satisfaction, there were two events that helped me to resume my course again: losing a large part of my material goods, and the death of my mother-in-law.

The Loss of Material Goods

As I reached my professional goals in the field of computer systems, I began to focus more on the accumulation of material goods. I had this misconception that success is measured by what we have. By 2008, when the United States experienced a crisis in the real estate market, Catherine and I had bought three properties with the idea of later selling two of them and paying off the one we would keep.

In order to acquire them, I worked a lot of overtime hours. I remember that I gave technical support to other companies after my regular full-time job and on several occasions, I had to sacrifice going on vacation with our three children. I thought that, in a short time, we would be able to enjoy our own house and family activities.

Unfortunately, this did not happen as we had planned. The economic bubble burst and the prices of the houses, which were already overpriced, began to fall dramatically. When we decided to sell both investment houses, people did not want to buy them because they were afraid, and the prices fell far below the value of our debt with the bank. In conclusion, in a few months those two properties were lost. The banks did not refinance the mortgage, as there was a large supply of houses for rent and no demand. It was difficult to keep up with the payments. All our effort, money, overtime, and vacation time with our children were gone right in front of our eyes.

All of this led to a severe stress situation. I could not sleep, I felt depressed ,and I was overwhelmed with guilt over the time I had not enjoyed with my children. Incredibly, Catherine was always very calm and was my emotional support during those stormy times. After a few months, looking at everything from another perspective, I could understand that my real wealth was my family and that it didn't matter where we lived as long as we were together. The day I understood that, everything changed for us. I could see that I was veering off course, focusing on something that was getting me nowhere and was not aligned with what I would do in the future.

My Mother-In-Law's Death

In 2012, my mother-in-law's health had begun to deteriorate, but without us suspecting a fatal outcome. A misdiagnosed illness led her to receive the wrong treatment, which did nothing to help her get better.

Her hospitalization supposedly due to dehydration, motivated Catherine, our children, and me to travel to Peru with the intention of lifting her spirits. We never imagined that this would be our farewell.

Two days after our arrival in Lima, my mother-in-law suffered a generalized infection. The doctors told us that there was nothing to be done and that it was only a matter of time. We couldn't believe it. Predicting what was to come, even though we had not told her anything about her situation, my mother-in-law began to say goodbye to each of us, telling us how much she loved us. After three days, she passed away surrounded by all of us.

I had to return to the United States because I could no longer take time off work. Catherine and our children stayed a few more days, making the necessary arrangements. A few days after Catherine returned to Charlotte, I found a book near my bedside table. It was "Many Lives Many Masters" by doctor and psychiatrist Brian Weiss; the same book my father had read and told me about when I was in my twenties. Once again, it came to me. Once again, the universe was making sure I received it.

I was not used to reading. I only read technology books when I had to learn a new operating system or study for a certification. When I picked up Weiss' book and read the first page, something made me continue reading the second and third pages and, without realizing it, I finished this book in one day. Nothing like this had ever happened to me before.

In this book, the author tells of his experience with a patient named Catherine, whose traumas and phobias came from a past life. He says that at all times he thought the young woman was hallucinating, but he found the level of detail in describing those supposed reincarnations incredible. During the months he had hypnosis sessions with her, Weiss began receiving messages from light beings while Catherine was in a hypnotic trance. This is similar to what has happened to me during my own sessions.

At the end of the book, I was amazed at the experiences I had shared. It was at this point that I decided that this was what I wanted to do. I wanted to learn regressive hypnosis, take people into past lives to get information, and help them heal.

The book, which belonged to my mother-in-law, looked almost new. We don't know if she ever read it, but we assumed she did, since she used to read two or three books at a time. If I think about it, and knowing that coincidences do not exist, my mother-in-law had bought that book - without knowing it - so that sooner or later it would come into my hands.

Her death caused a major change in our lives and brought Catherine into a state of depression. She felt that the process of life was meaningless, being born, living, suffering, and dying in those conditions. What was the purpose of life? Even though I believed in reincarnation, I did not know what to say to her to comfort her, to give her the peace she needed, to get the answers to all the questions she could never ask her mother, to understand why she had lived certain events with her.

"I did not go in search of that knowledge and answers. They came to me on their own," Catherine said some time later. She was referring to what happened a few years later, when I had already started practicing hypnosis, and my mother-in-law communicated with me through one of my clients in a trance. That time she was able to give her the answers my wife had always been waiting for, to help her close her grieving cycle with love and give her a better under-standing of how the spirit world works.

Once I finished reading Weiss' book, I could see that I identified with his work and everything he had written. I could also understand why this work had come to me for the second time. The universe was making sure that I aligned myself with my purpose. Also, it was telling me that it was time to start what I had come to do in this reincarnation. That same day in 2013, I decided to learn about regressive hypnosis. I turned on the computer and started looking for information on the Internet, and that's how I came to Aurelio Mejia and Dolores Cannon.

Aurelio Mejía

As soon as I finished reading the book, I figured that, unlike the time when my father had first mentioned it, it would be easier for me to find websites and videos about it. That's how I found the YouTube channel of Colombian hypnotherapist, Aurelio Mejia.

In his videos, I was able to see him performing regressions to past lives, focusing mostly on memories of his clients' current lives. Meanwhile, he guided them through that traumatic event in order to remove the negative emotion associated with it. I noticed that his clients would go into past lives only in the event that their problem or symptom had originated in that life.

I was struck by his simplicity, his occurrences, and that he always knew what to say at the precise moment when his clients were reliving a traumatic event during the trance. I also noticed the time he took to talk to the camera and explain what was happening and why he applied this or that technique. It was very enriching.

At that time, I was still working as a systems engineer for a company and the day after finishing the book, my vacation began. I began to watch his videos one after another. I spent hours in front of the computer in awe of everything that was happening in those sessions; from past lives, communication with spirits and spirits attached to his clients, the use of stories with hidden messages to help change behaviors, to communication with spirit guides, who conveyed messages of love and hope.

Aurelio would do all of this while getting up from his chair for coffee, pausing to give an explanation to the camera, or while talking to his client's companion. He could do everything at once with incredible ease, as if it were the most normal thing in the world. That is how I watched each one of his hundreds of videos - at that time, he had a little over two thousand on his first channel - and without realizing it, I spent almost a week watching them. I knew them by heart and, although I was struggling to understand his technique, I understood that each session is different so it was necessary to know how to improvise and adapt to it.

After a week, I was motivated to give him a call. I never thought he would answer me, as someone who is that well known and busy. To my surprise, Aurelio answered. I introduced myself and told him. I was a big fan of his videos, which he appreciated enormously. I also asked him if he taught classes, and if he planned to travel to the United States. He answered that he didn't have any plans at the moment. For my part, I couldn't go see him either because of my work commitment.

This led me to look for other people from whom I could receive training in regressive hypnosis. I remember my cousin, Malena, telling me about hypnotherapist Dolores Cannon, who had been practicing the Quantum Healing Hypnosis Technique (QHHT) for over 40 years, and I would later learn directly from her. Later I will talk about Dolores.

It wasn't until about a year later that I was able to arrange for Aurelio to visit Charlotte. At that time, I had been practicing QHHT for a year after taking the level one and two classes with Dolores Cannon, getting good results despite my short experience, and the challenges that any apprentice faces in the field of hypnosis. Despite having taken people to past lives, like my son Christian, who was my first volunteer, I felt that something was missing. There were certain situations that presented themselves in the sessions for which I did not have the necessary tools. At that time, I was still following Aurelio's YouTube channel and didn't rule out learning his technique.

In 2014, my wife, Catherine, learned that Aurelio was planning to visit some cities in the United States to facilitate sessions. She herself was interested in having a hypnosis session with him, and was even willing to drive the ten hours to Miami for the meeting. At that point, I assumed that it would be difficult to make an appointment, and I was not wrong. The contact person in Miami informed us that the thirty slots were already taken and that there were another thirty people on the waiting list, so he advised us to call the contact person in Connecticut, but the response was the same.

I think the following is the best example of how destiny has things ready for us. When she couldn't get an appointment, Catherine thought we should call Aurelio's assistant to ask her about the requirements to host him in our city. I remember I just looked at her and smiled as I thought that option would be impossible as well. I was very surprised when we called his assistant, María Eugenia, and she told us that the organizer of the third city Aurelio was going to visit had just cancelled for personal reasons. We told her that we were interested in hosting him, and that we had the necessary facilities so that he could facilitate sessions in our house. Over the course of the next few days, we scheduled and planned Aurelio's visit to Charlotte, where he would stay for seven days facilitating sessions.

We were more than excited. I could not believe the opportunity that was presenting itself to me. As soon as Aurelio posted about his visit to Charlotte with our contact information, the spots were filled in three days, and we had about thirty people on the waiting list. It was unbelievable.

During my learning and initiation into the practice of QHHT, I formed new friendships with colleagues who were performing the same technique. Among the people I most esteem and admire are Alba Weinman and Genoveva Calleja, with whom I maintain a beautiful friendship and constant contact. It was to them, by chance and with Aurelio's permission, that I invited them to Charlotte. Only Genoveva was able to join, since Alba had a trip scheduled.

When I first met Aurelio at the airport, I saw a simple, kind and humorous person who radiated very positive energy. He talked to me as if he had known me all my life and I felt the same way about him. Today I have no doubt that our meeting and my learning his technique, was something we had agreed on before reincarnating. There could not be any other explanation for such synchronicity.

Over the next six days, Aurelio facilitated thirty-eight hypnosis sessions in our home, from which Genoveva and I learned invaluable lessons, not only in the field of hypnosis, but also personally. We were aware of his human quality, which went beyond his videos. But actually having him with us, we learned from his simplicity, humility and his gift of service.

The first day was full of emotions and expectations. Aurelio facilitated six sessions and I already felt exhausted. The maximum number of sessions I had done in one day was two, and only in extreme cases. He lived and breathed hypnosis. Everything he explained to us he did without mysticism and without complicating himself too much.

At the moment of teaching, there are no manuals or rigid structures for him.

During the sessions, his mind would go at a hundred miles an hour, tying up loose ends and putting together the puzzle of his client's life, while he visited past events in this life and others in a matter of minutes. His training in the field of electronics and computing in his native Medellín, Colombia, had contributed greatly to this facility, as he saw the human being as a computer with a central processing unit equivalent to our brain.

While it is true that Genoveva and I were knowledgeable about regressive hypnosis, we learned from him additional tools that would take our practice of hypnosis to the next level. Aurelio began by letting us witness the sessions while he explained what he was doing and made some notes in his notebook. By the second day, he was allowing us to do the induction of the person and then take them out of the trance, taking turns. In the following days, he let us participate more in the sessions, navigating through memories, using role changes, and even talking to the spirits that were presenting themselves. By the last day, we had a complete idea of the order and techniques used.

I remember that, in the few minutes in between sessions, we would ask him questions and he would answer them all. Today I think that, more than learning his technique, I learned to put my ego aside and understand that we do not heal anyone, but that it is our clients who heal themselves while we guide them. I also learned to take away the mysticism of the techniques, not to fear their complexity, and not to pay attention to the labels or diagnoses that had been put on the clients -depression, schizophrenia, fibromyalgia, bipolarity, among others- since those were only symptoms whose origin could be psychosomatic and different for each one.

Seven days later, it was time to say goodbye to Aurelio. Genoveva was living in New York at the time and would have the opportunity to continue learning from him for another week during his visit to

Connecticut. For me, it was the end of an incredible learning experience with an exceptional teacher and human being. I did not see him again until a few months later in Mexico, during a conference organized on his behalf, and then a year later when he returned to Charlotte to facilitate more sessions.

It was on that second trip that I would have the opportunity to refine his technique. Even though I had been practicing Introspective Hypnosis for a year and many people had had sessions with me since Aurelio included me on his website and in his YouTube videos, there was still more knowledge to be gained.

Dolores Cannon

As I mentioned above, not being able to learn Aurelio Mejia's technique, I came upon the name of Dolores Cannon thanks to my cousin. The American hypnotherapist, who specialized in past life regressions, had been practicing hypnosis for several years, and she had begun teaching the Quantum Healing Hypnosis Technique a few years earlier.

Cannon is considered one of the best exponents of past life regression through the use of hypnosis. Her career in this field spanned almost fifty years until the day she passed away in 2014. Her first experience with reincarnations was in 1968, when a doctor from the Texas Naval Base asked her to help a patient with eating disorders and obesity. During the session, the patient began to describe scenes from Chicago in the 1920's. That is how she and her husband, Johnny, began to develop their own technique of regression to past lives, at a time when this concept was not yet known.

When I visited her website, I read that she gave workshops online and in person. I didn't think twice about it and, in the following days, I took the QHHT Level 1 course, which took about ten days after my working hours. In that course, based on videos from a live class, Dolores explained her technique and guided us step by step to understand it. What I valued most about the class were the stories and personal experiences she had accumulated over the years through thousands of sessions. She had the gift of captivating the audience with her stories. Not for nothing had she been very successful in writing and publishing her books.

I remember that, when I finished the course, I was eager to start practicing, but the hardest part was getting volunteers to let me hypnotize them. My friends and acquaintances avoided the subject so I asked my son, Christian, to be my first volunteer. After thinking about it, he agreed. I had never put anyone in a trance before and I really didn't think it would work, so I didn't even record the session. We did the session in his room and, once the induction was over, I asked him to travel in time and space in search of a past life, which he had no problem finding. I began by asking him for a description of his body and clothing, starting with his feet. With a different tone of voice and slightly displeased, he began to describe himself as a man in a suit lying on a street with old cars on either side. He had apparently been the victim of a vehicle collision in that area. I continued to ask him questions, but my lack of experience led me to believe that he was making up the story to make me feel good. I was even tempted to touch him and tell him to stop playing, but I felt that it would not be appropriate to do that if he was really in a trance.

The session lasted a few minutes and, as I thought it wasn't working, I decided to take him out of the trance and end the session. When I asked him to open his eyes, he apologized for having fallen asleep. I started laughing and asked him not to play with me and he said "What are you talking about, Dad? I fell asleep." I told him that this was impossible because he had talked to me for thirty minutes and had given me many details of a supposed past life. At that moment, he was the one who told me not to joke. We had to call Catherine to confirm my words.

I still remember the comedy of the situation. I had put someone in a trance for the first time and it was so deep that he didn't remember anything when he came out of it. Due to lack of confidence in myself, I had not recorded the session. Christian had turned out to be one of those people who, when they go to past lives, becomes that character. His tone of voice and expressions changed during those moments. Over the next few months, I would continue to learn and practice QHHT. Since at that time getting volunteers was not easy, my cousin Malena organized sessions with a group of interested people from Miami and I traveled to facilitate sessions there. The results were excellent. Several of the volunteers visited past lives and obtained the information they needed at the time.

The Jewish Child in the Gas Chamber

During that series of practice sessions in Miami, one of the cases that touched my heart was that of Jessy, who went to a past life where she was a Jewish boy during World War II. He told how he was hiding from the German soldiers along with other children in the home of people who were helping them. Jessy also told me that when he was caught, he was taken to a kind of room with gray walls where there were other Jews as well.

> **Antonio**: I want you to move forward in time, so that you can tell me if they find you or not.
>
> **Child**: It's a gray place.
>
> **A**: And the other children who were with you?
>
> **C**: I don't know.
>
> **A**: Why are you in that place? Did you go there alone?
>
> **C**: No.
>
> **A**: Did they find you?
>
> **C**: Yes. There are other people in this place.
>
> **A**: Are they Jews too?
>
> **C**: Yes. There is a priest too.

A: Jewish?

C: No. He tells me he is Catholic. He also tells me that every-thing will pass.

A: Look around you. Where do they sleep?

At that point, Jessy began to feel like she was suffocating. She put her hands around her neck as she struggled for air. What SHE was feeling during the trance was the same HE felt in that past life, when she was that Jewish boy. Without a doubt, the place he was describing to me was a gas chamber, where he and others were taken to be killed. I guess that's why the priest was telling the boy that everything was going to pass.

I asked Jessy to move forward to the moment he was leaving his body. I told him it wouldn't affect him, that he should continue to tell me what was happening. Again, he began to breathe normally. When I asked him what he needed to learn in that short life, he said to have compassion. The boy had felt compassion both for the others who were with him and for the priest who was with him. They had all died in that place.

My learning and practice of QHHT continued. I could see that each client who came to me presented a new challenge and a higher level of complexity. In a short time, I also realized that I was never sent a session that I could not facilitate, as the challenges increased as my knowledge and confidence increased.

I am sure that, if my first volunteers had not gone into a trance, I might have thought that hypnosis was not for me, and I would not be writing this book today. My guides sent me people who easily went into that state while I was practicing, as if to encourage me and con-firm that the regression did work. Gradually I received more complex cases and people with all kinds of blockages. Today I understand that this was the only way to perfect my technique, gain experience, and prepare for what the future held for me.

Almost a year after taking the QHHT Level 1 course, I traveled to Arkansas to take the Level 2 course with Dolores Cannon in person. Not only did I have the privilege of meeting her, but also of receiving knowledge and advice directly from her as she told us about her experiences. It was in this class that I met many who, like me, had gone through a tough process before getting there. During the days we spent together, after each class, we had the opportunity to share and get to know each other better. I discovered that many of us had been torn in two and that, little by little, we had learned to heal ourselves; so now we wanted to help others heal themselves as well.

In this workshop, I met Alba Weinman, a friend and colleague with whom I have a friendship today. Alba and I grew up together in the field of hypnosis. From that date until today, we have shared the experiences of our sessions, given each other support whenever we needed it, exchanged techniques, and taught each other new ones as we put them into practice. Catherine has always supported our friendship and understood our long conversations on the phone. We have both given each other the support we need to continue to evolve in the field of hypnosis.

During one of the Introspective Hypnosis classes we would teach years later, one of the assistants, who was in a trance, channeled a light being, who said that Alba and I had come together to teach how to help others with love. That would be confirmation of what we had suspected for some time.

Through Alba, I met Genoveva Calleja, whom I spoke of above, and with whom I have had a similar experience of constant support and mutual learning. It was because of her that I was encouraged to take Michael Newton's Life Between Lives course. In this way, my circle of friends and colleagues was transformed and began to take shape. Without the interaction and support we provide to each other, it would have been much more difficult to continue this journey.

Michael Newton

Although I did not have the opportunity to meet American hypnotherapist Michael Newton in person, I decided to list him as one of my teachers in hypnosis because his books and the Life Between Lives technique he developed have influenced my practice and the style in which I facilitate my hypnosis sessions tremendously.

By the end of the year 2018, and at the suggestion and insistence of my friend and colleague Genoveva Calleja, who had already taken the course and felt that it was the next step in our learning, I decided to register for the workshop given by the Newton Institute, located in the United States. This course is designed for therapists with experience in the field of hypnosis, but especially in the field of regressive hypnosis. In order to take the class, you have to fulfill and demonstrate that you have a series of requirements, such as hours of training and experience in hypnosis. Once all the required information has been submitted, the Newton Institute takes a few weeks to inform whether one is accepted or not.

The Life Between Lives technique is not just about regression to past lives, but about using a past life as an entrance to the spiritual world, our true home. This is meant to help spirit - our client - to navigate through its memories, through everything that happens before reincarnation. Through the state of super consciousness, the person will not only be able to understand what he or she planned to learn in the current reincarnation, but also how the current lessons relate to those of previous lives. Also, they will be able to have contact with their soul group and spirit guide and receive suggestions from wise or advanced spirits. All of this occurs if the person is authorized to receive such information, as it can be blocked by their guide if it could be counterproductive.

In my years of experience, I have concluded that this technique is not for just anyone, nor is it for any practitioner of hypnosis. To begin with, it is necessary to go into a very deep trance and be ready to hear the information being sought, because it could affect the learning plan being laid out. Nor is it designed for all practitioners of hypnosis since, with this technique, we are at the service of spirit guides and the council of the elders. To be an instrument of them, it is necessary to work on ourselves previously, to have an open mind and heart, and the right intentions. It is fundamental to show respect for these beings of light.

Genoveva and the instructors had already mentioned that this technique worked first on ourselves, but I never imagined the magnitude. The course lasted six days and we were twelve participants, of which seven were Spanish speaking. Some of us lived in the United States and others had traveled from other countries.

Each of us came with previous knowledge of hypnosis, as well as our own techniques and styles. During those six days, group and couples' exercises took me out of my comfort zone. No matter how much I knew, I had to learn to let go of my ego completely. The universe knew what it was doing, because now I understand that this process was necessary to establish a communication with the spirit world.

When the class was over, I was required to facilitate five practice sessions in order to be certified. I thought it was going to be easy. At least, that is what my ego thought. I thought it was just a matter of calling those clients who had already had a session with me and had gone into a deep trance, to offer them practice sessions, and that getting certified would take only a few weeks.

The universe had another plan for me. It would take me a total of nineteen sessions to put together the five sessions required for certification. During those sessions, the Life Between Lives technique took care of my ego, my humbleness, and most of all, my patience. I learned to surrender to the universe and to accept that, as much as I wanted my volunteer to enter the spirit world, this depended only on what the guides deemed necessary. As Genoveva once told me, "The day you get certified, you're going to feel as if you've been accepted to college." She was not wrong.

Hashtra and Her Guide

One of the first Life Between Lives sessions in which I experienced blockage from the guides, was in Luz's session. She had agreed to volunteer for a practice session for my certification.

Luz is a simple woman, who I met when she and her husband had sessions with Aurelio while he was in Charlotte, in which I also participated. I knew she would be an excellent candidate because she was one of those people who would go into a deep trance and then not remember anything about what took place in the session. That day, she brought a list of questions with which I sought to better understand who she was as a spirit and what her purpose was in this life.

Already in the session, while communicating with her guide who coincidentally had the same name, we asked her opinion about the performance of Hashtra – Luz's spiritual and eternal name- in her past life as Marli. The guide told us that, in that reincarnation, there were two goals: kindness and humility. Hashtra, in Marli's life, had passed the test of kindness, but not that of humility, because she had placed too much importance to material goods.

When I asked her how many lives she had been trying to learn about humility, the guide answered seven. She also let us know that Hashtra, in her life as Luz, was doing well. When I asked the guide if it was time to take her to the next station in the spirit world, she said not yet, and told us that Luz had one more life to live on this planet. I asked her a few more questions to get more information, but she said she couldn't tell us more.

During the rest of the session, I saw how the guide was very careful with the information she gave Hashtra, as she did not want to affect in any way, the life she had left live. Even when we visited the council of the elders, where she received a lot of information, they reiterated that she had only one more reincarnation left on this planet. I also felt that they were prudent with the information they were giving her.

Following the teachings of Michael Newton, I tried to get the information that was being blocked along the stations in the spirit world we visited, but the result was the same. Finally, I decided to take her to the place where we choose the body we will have in the next reincarnation. I wanted Luz to understand why she had chosen her current body.

> **Antonio**: Hashtra, let's go to the moment when you choose the female body you are going to have in the life of Luz. Let's see why you choose that body. You let me know when you are there.

> **Hashtra**: I'm here.

> **A**: What does this place look like where you choose the body and sex that you are going to have?

> **H**: I can't get through -she answered, shaking her head back and forth in a voice of frustration.

I asked her to repeat a paragraph asking her guide to give me permission to access that information, to trust me because I was there to help her.

> **A**: Try to cross over now and see what happens. Describe everything you are seeing.

> **H**: I'm walking -she said, breathing fast and moving her head from side to side.

> **A**: Did they let you through?

> **H**: No, I'm just walking around that energy.

> **A**: See if there is an entrance.

> **H**: No, it's very thick glass. It's an energy that I can't get through.

> **A**: Do you feel that this energy has consciousness?

> **H**: Yes.

A: Can you lend your mind and lips to communicate with it?

H: I am afraid. I am very small and that energy is very big.

A: I'll ask questions and you repeat what it answers, is that okay?

At that moment, I turned to that energy, to that consciousness, to give us permission to pass and thus help Hashtra to have a better understanding of the lessons of her current life as Light, and of the next one.

A: What is your response?

H: She won't let me pass because I have to complete this life. She says that I cannot know what will come in my next reincarnation.

With this response, it had become clear that no further information would be given to her as it could affect her performance in this or her next reincarnation. Apparently, as stated in the book, "Destiny of Souls," written by Michael Newton, information about future lives can be accessed from this station.

After a few minutes, we concluded the session. Luz did not remember anything she had said to me in the two hours she had been in a deep hypnotic trance.

José Luis Cabouli

At the end of 2019, and at the suggestion of my friend and colleague, Ery Cervantes, I decided to attend a congress in Mexico where Argentinean doctor, José Luis Cabouli, creator of the Past Life Therapy (TVP) technique, would be present. Although I did not know much about him, Ery had told me about the effectiveness of his technique and the ease with which he brought his clients into an expanded state of consciousness in order to work with different traumas. This caught my attention because, up to that point, I had the idea that for someone to go into a deep trance, a good hypnotic induction was needed.

The concept that most surprised me was Cabouli's presentation about soul entrapment. For him, the soul is timeless; that is, that the soul does not understand time, since for it, everything happens in the now. Listening to him speak, I felt that I had a master in front of me, not only because of his knowledge, but also because of his simplicity, humility, and openness to share everything he knew.

When it came time to ask for volunteers for the demonstration, I was able to see first-hand what they experienced during their sessions. I was more than surprised, not only to see the person go into a trance without induction, but to see what they accomplished after working with his technique.

That's how I was encouraged to register for the TVP course he taught in Spain, in February, 2020. It was in this class, taught by him, that I learned a series of additional and invaluable techniques that I use today in my practice, such as working around symptoms that my clients brought to the session, to locate them in the body in order to associate them to something they are familiar with, and from there take them to a parallel experience, to another life, where there was something pending, something they were not able to complete then.

Dr. Cabouli maintains that when in a past life, we have not been aware of what was happening to us during the death of our body on a physical, emotional, and mental level, part of our energy and our soul gets trapped in that experience, reliving it over and over again and causing the symptom in our current body. This idea, based on the principle of the timelessness of the soul, maintains that the spirit is the same and never dies, bringing the symptoms of that reincarnation to the current body.

During the eight days of the first module, we all learned a lot, including how to work with post mortem entrapment and entrapment in the womb. I was able to confirm not only Cabouli's level of knowledge, but also his human quality. I had definitely made the right decision in signing up for his workshop.

Once in Charlotte, I began to use the techniques I had learned with surprising results. Dolores Cannon's QHHT had taught me how to disconnect people from dramatic situations related to the death of the body in a past life. And, following Dr. Cabouli's teachings, I was able to allow my clients to feel everything again while helping them become aware of what was happening on a physical, emotional, and mental level. This newly acquired procedure would cause almost immediate relief for my clients, although it would also create a stir among my colleagues and students, who were not yet able to understand the concept.

Cabouli's teachings allowed me to refine my techniques and approach to working with the symptoms my clients bring with them. Now I not only asked them to disconnect from traumatic events to avoid suffering. Quite the contrary, now I also led them to feel everything they had felt at that moment, but from three aspects: physical, mental, and emotional. This would be the secret ingredient that would lead them to self-healing from the trauma, accompanied also by the understanding of what each of these aspects caused in them and prevented them from doing in their current reincarnation.

The Techniques and the Soul Map

Above I have mentioned the preparation and teachers I have had up to the time I am writing this book. I am of the idea that we never stop learning, that there is always room for more knowledge and experience. I know that in the future I will learn other techniques that I will later incorporate into my hypnosis sessions, thus changing the style of the sessions and the experience my clients will have through them.

Although I have mentioned four techniques from four teachers, the knowledge is all one, as these are always present in my sessions, and I use them according to what is presented to me. My practice and style have been transformed by adapting each one of them to my own experiences and methods, which I have been implementing over the years.

I always respect what clients request. If they come to me asking for a specific technique, that will be the one I give him. I believe it is important to respect their free will and work around it. If we imagine that the soul has a map that takes us to different times, places, dimensions, and realities, I think the four techniques help me to navigate each aspect efficiently.

For example, the Quantum Healing Hypnosis Technique specializes in going through past lives. It is in them that the person has a better understanding of the patterns they face in their current reincarnation, as we bring many of them with us.

In addition, the client gains a better understanding of the lessons learned or not learned in that life, thus allowing them to understand that the situation they currently face is simply the same test that is being repeated. This motivates them to take responsibility for it in order to pass it.

During the navigation through past lives, you will encounter people who are also living in the current reincarnation. Let's remember that we are part of a group of spirits that reincarnate from life to life exchanging roles. Knowing that this or that person was with us before and now also, helps us to better understand the circumstance we are going through for them or with them. This also helps us to understand what we have to learn.

Another aspect that QHHT offers is contact with the Higher Self, that part of us that is connected to the spirit world. Our Higher Self knows everything about us, whether in this life or other lives, and is the one who can give us advice and a greater explanation of what we are living.

On the other hand, Introspective Hypnosis, based on Aurelio Mejia's Hipnosis Introspectiva's (Introspective Hypnosis) technique, focuses on the issues of this life, on what is affecting us now, especially psychosomatic symptoms caused by repressed emotions, such as depression, grief, anguish, pain, problems in relationships with other people and, behavior patterns, among others. It guides the person to the root cause of their symptoms and traumas, analyzing the event from another perspective, to eliminate the negative emotion associated with it.

I have added other tools and procedures to this technique myself as I have learned and evolved in the field. And, in turn, Introspective Hypnosis employs different elements, such as forgiveness therapy. Ericksonian hypnosis, which follows the teachings of Milton Erickson, consists of using stories and metaphors with hidden messages to induce psycho-emotional situations without the loss of consciousness, regression to past lives, or assistance to spirits. In the search for the origin of such symptoms, the client may visit a sad memory in this or other reincarnations where some event there caused it. Understanding that this situation belongs to another body, the client decides to withdraw the associated symptom that his or her spirit caused in the current body.

The origin of certain symptoms can also be caused by spirit attachments. These are lost or confused souls that decided not to go into the light. We must remember that we all have free will in the spirit world, while we are incarnated, and when our body dies. The mission of Introspective hypnosis is also to help those souls. There are times when it is necessary to give them therapy using the same tools that we use with our clients. Our goal should be to help them go to the light or source.

As for José Luis Cabouli's Past Life Therapy (TVP), it focuses even more on psychosomatic symptoms, using them as the thread that will lead us to another experience, another life. Its basis is the principle of the timelessness of the soul, which holds that past lives are not really in the past, since they are simultaneous and occur in the now. If we start from the point that the spirit does not understand time and that everything is happening now, we can understand why the symptom that comes from a past reincarnation accompanies us in the present. Because of this, technically, TVP is not a regression or a journey back in time. It is rather a therapy to help make conscious what is unconscious for our clients. It is this that will guide them to the root cause of the symptom they are suffering from.

Life Between Lives focuses on navigating through the memories of the spiritual world, through everything that happens before we reincarnate.

This technique, developed by Michael Newton, helps the person to understand that we are eternal spirits and as such we have our own identity and spiritual name. LBL helps us to understand that we are not the body we occupy. This is just a vehicle, like many others we have had in other lifetimes, that our spirit uses to experience different aspects of life on planet Earth.

During this type of session, the person establishes contact with their spirit guide, a being of light and love who receives us when our body dies. He is the best therapist for our clients as he knows everything about them and is always available to evaluate our performance in this and other lives, to remind us of the lessons we came to learn, or simply to keep us from going off our learning path.

During the exploration of the spiritual world, the person contacts his or her spiritual group, the council of the elders, the station where they choose the body and other ones. All of this allows for a better understanding of who he is and what he is here for.

By using the LBL technique, I realized that I was putting myself at the service of the spirit guides and the council of the elders, spirits who help us evaluate our performance in past lives and our spiritual evolution. I always say that LBL is not a technique for just any client or just any therapist. From the client's point of view, one needs to enter into a deep trance, usually the beta state of mind. On the therapist's side, he must not only know hypnosis, but also navigate through past lives, put the ego aside, have the heartfelt intention to help the client with love, and compassion to understand that the session is not about him, but about his client, his spiritual group, his guidance and the advice of the wise.

An LBL session is a wonderful experience that allows us to return to our original essence, to remember who we are and why we are here. As I said earlier, many people are blocked by their spiritual guides when they are not yet ready to have the understanding of what they are going through.

The four techniques I have mentioned allow me to cover all aspects of the soul map: the past, the present, and the timeless state (the spirit world). This has made it possible for me to better guide my clients in their search for answers, the root cause of their symptoms, and situations in their current life that afflict them. In addition, they can allow themselves to evaluate their spiritual evolution, to begin making necessary changes, and to obtain the maximum learning during their current reincarnation.

Something that has characterized me in life is a constant search for knowledge; my investigative spirit. I was always trying different techniques and inductions, and I was never afraid to try all this new stuff during my sessions. If there is something that I would like to be remembered for in the future, I would want it to be by always staying out of my comfort zone, by looking for a better way of doing things and getting results, by questioning and wanting to recreate what I learned from books and teachers, before assuming that as true.

To better understand what I have just explained, I will mention something I state in the Introspective Hypnosis courses I teach:

Navigating a past life, current life, or life between lives, is an art. It's not just about asking questions to gather information about them and passing it on to our clients to see what they do with it. The idea, and our goal, is to detect the patterns that have been presenting from other lives and associate them to the events experienced in the current life, in order to help our clients draw their own conclusions, motivating them to correct their behavior and actions.

As a metaphor, what a client who comes to us for help is telling us, is the following:

When I was created as energy, I had the complete puzzle of my spirit. As I started reincarnating, I lost some of the pieces. That is why I now feel incomplete. I need you to help me find them.

Our role is to navigate through past lives, memories of the present reincarnation, and even the space between lives ,to find those pieces and make our client feel whole again.

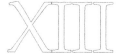

THE COINCIDENCES

Despite using the word coincidence, today I know that they do not exist. Everything happens as planned, even when we use our free will. Remember the example I gave several pages ago about multiple-choice exams. We choose only one answer from those presented, but, in the spiritual world, it does not really matter which one we select because they will always teach us something. There is no wrong answer. Let's think of these possible answers as contingency plans, not A to E, but A to infinity, where nothing happens by chance or is left to chance.

Based on this principle, we could assume that nothing I have experienced was by chance. If I look back in time and analyze the journey I have made, I realize that, to do what I do today, there was a work plan carefully elaborated by my spirit. There were no loose ends in it, because everything had to happen this way.

If, at the age of eighteen, a psychic had told me that I was going to live in the United States, that I would be a systems engineer providing technical support in English and Spanish, and that, by the time I reached my forties, I would be practicing hypnosis in both languages and then teaching my technique, I would not have believed him. I am honest in saying that I always felt in search of something more, but I never imagined I would be where I am now.

The reality is that every time Catherine and I made plans for the future, the universe would take us to another shore, and we would end up in a different, but always better, destination than the original plan. We planned to have our own company and live comfortably from our income, since my worst nightmare was having to work sitting at a desk until my retirement day. However, the last twenty-five years I have spent doing exactly that. I now understand that scenario had a why and a wherefore. Today it is easy for me to locate the points that influenced my preparation.

My Parents

If in the future I was to connect and establish a relationship with my clients and students who attended my classes, I had to be able to express myself and reach out to them. I had, above all, to project my spirit and my intention to help through love. I grew up in a home with marked contrasts. Through my mother, I learned to connect with all kinds of people because she had the ability to engage in friendly conversation with the more introverted, moody, and uncompromising individuals. I remember her going to my school to talk to my teachers. I would see the strictest and most serious of them turn into sweet little kittens from listening to her talk. My mother has that gift, the gift of speech, the gift of reaching out to people. As she often says, "everyone has their sweet spot, it's just a matter of knowing how to reach out to them." She also taught me about service and spirituality.

From my father I learned about metaphysics. He always shared with me the concepts he learned from the books he read. He was a tireless fighter who taught me to never give up and not be afraid to fall. By his example, I learned how to get up from every difficult situation in life.

Among the many virtues of each one, are the gift of speech, patience, love and the drive to follow that I apply every day in my life.

This is what motivates me to keep learning and advancing in my spiritual evolution.

The English Language

If I had the responsibility of facilitating sessions not only for Hispanics who could not speak English, but also for native English speakers, it made sense that I should learn this language. I needed it to communicate and to be able to conduct a session, in which you improvise without following scripts. I also had to speak English fluently in order to share knowledge with people from different parts of the world. This was definitely a requirement.

From kindergarten to third grade, I was in an American-Peruvian school where 95% of the teaching was in English. Although I was able to learn the basic vocabulary, when I reached third grade I began to have problems with my studies. I felt that I did not understand and was easily distracted. I think that today that would be diagnosed as attention deficit disorder/hyperactivity disorder.

It was at the end of that grade that my parents decided to move me to a Catholic school, where English did not represent even one percent of the school curriculum. At that point, we could say that the plan to learn English had failed. But, as I mentioned before, there are always contingency plans. I had to learn English and there was no way around it.

Years later, in 1986, I entered college and met Catherine. After the second semester was over, she asked me about my plans for the summer and I answered that I thought I would just be on vacation. Catherine suggested that we enroll in an institute to learn English. I remember my answer was a definite no. I told her about my experience as a child and the trauma I had with that language. She only had to tell me that she would register anyway, I was encouraged to do so as well. The truth is that it was all a result of my youthful jealousy. That had been the contingency plan. I didn't learn it as a child, but I learned it when I was nineteen for fear of losing Catherine.

Catherine and I attended together, although she decided after the fifth month not to attend anymore. I stayed for three years, studying. The basic knowledge acquired during my childhood helped me to learn it more easily in my youth.

The Study of Computer Science

I think that, in order to facilitate regressive hypnosis sessions correctly, the practitioner must have the patience and the ability to find the root cause or symptom through different access routes. This is especially necessary during the navigation of past lives, the analysis after each one of them, and the navigation of the spirit world.

During our two-year return to Peru in 1997, I decided to study computer science. I was very interested in computers and felt that I had the ability to work with them. It was then that I became a Microsoft Certified Systems Engineer. I also learned how to assemble and repair computers.

I was amazed at how easily I could detect where the problem was located in the interconnection of a computer network, being able to find what others had been unable to. The same thing happened when it was my turn to assemble or repair computers, or to detect the fault in the operating system. I realized that my brain had been trained to follow a logical sequence and structure in the search for the problem, in order to reach the origin of the fault.

This knowledge served me well when facilitating hypnosis sessions. The human mind and the spirit map work in the same way -at least that is how I perceive it- and under the same premise. I see the person as a computer, having a central processing unit (CPU) and a storage unit full of information and programs that have been installed from the moment of birth.

When it comes to navigating past reincarnations, I see the spirit as a computer network, where this is the central processing unit and the past lives are the computers interconnected to the network, affecting each other at all times.

But how is this possible? Why do we say that past lives are interconnected and affect us all the time? The answer is simple. Under the premise that time does not exist, the soul does not understand the past, present, and future, for it is only the interpretation that the human brain has given time to be able to understand it. The reality is that only the now exists. For the soul, life is one with experiences in different bodies.

Because of what was explained in the previous paragraph, we can determine then that a past life is not past, but parallel or simultaneous, where everything that happens there, affects our body in this life, and everything that affects us in this life, affects those previous lives. Returning to the example of the computer network, let us imagine that a virus affects one of the machines. This would cause all the others connected to the network to be affected as well. If we think of an antivirus for the entire network, once installed on the main server, it will eliminate the virus from all other computers.

The Abandoned Beggar

To better understand this concept, I think it is useful to tell you the following case. Sabrina took my Introspective Hypnosis course. During the exercises and the demonstration of the inductions, I realized that she had a great ability to enter into a deep trance quickly. Upon seeing this, I asked her if she was interested in learning how to facilitate telepathic sessions in which one person is put into a trance, and then have them connect to a third person to work with them. In other words, it is like facilitating a hypnosis session for someone through a third person, surrogate, or substitute.

During this time, I established a friendship with Sabrina and we worked on a couple of telepathic sessions together. When it came time for me to get volunteers for my Life Between Lives certification, I immediately felt that she would be an excellent candidate. Sabrina had told me about a symptom that had afflicted her for many years, pain in her teeth. She had visited dentists and spent a lot of money on dental work, but the pain persisted. Her dentist had no explanation for it. Before starting the session, I asked her to put her intention in that affliction and ask her spiritual guide to show her information about it.

Already in a trance, Sabrina went to a life where she was an old man in rags named Raymond, who was on a dirt road near a castle-like building with high cement walls. When I asked Sabrina to continue describing what she saw, she told me in tears that she was touching her mouth and she had no teeth.

Antonio: Why don't you have teeth?

Raymond: I'm poor. They rotted and fell out because I didn't have money to fix them.

A: How do you fix the teeth there?

R: I don't know. I see rich people who have nice white teeth. Mine are black and I've had several taken out.

I felt that Sabrina had gone to the reincarnation where the root cause of her tooth pain was. I knew that by asking the right questions we would get the information she needed. As I asked more questions of Raymond in that life, he became more emotional and the conversation revolved around his bad teeth. He told me that he was living off the handouts people gave him when they saw him in that state.

R: I see well-dressed people passing by in carriages. I see men in elegant suits, but no one pays attention to me.

A: And how does that make you feel?

R: As if I didn't exist, alone and abandoned. I feel a lot of sadness inside me and that makes me not want to live anymore.

A: Raymond, were you always poor?

R: No.

Raymond told me that he was a farmer as a child. He helped with the cows and had nice teeth. He was thin, but strong, and he mostly took care of his animals. I asked him when he became poor and he said he had to sell the farm his father had left him because he didn't make enough money to support it, since people no longer bought the milk he sold. There was another person who produced more milk and butter at a better price, and since Raymond lived far away, people preferred to buy from that other vendor.

When I asked him to move forward to the time of his death, he described being in an alley. Some teenagers had stolen his mug with money and had kicked him so hard in the face that his jaw and skull had broken, causing his death. He was eighty-five years old.

Once out of his body, I asked Raymond to give me his impressions of the life that had just ended. He did not understand why his life had been so miserable and ended in such a sad way. On the other hand, he was relieved because he no longer felt the pain of his rotting teeth.

As he evaluated his life with his guide, the life that had recently ended, he said that he had allowed others to make him feel small and insignificant. He also indicated that, in the life as Sabrina, she too felt insignificant, when in fact she was very powerful. Sabrina and Raymond had allowed the monetary value assigned to them to affect them physically and emotionally. That's why, every time Sabrina went through difficult financial times, her spirit and body remembered Raymond's life, making those emotions and fears reflect as pain in her teeth.

This is a clear example of how our past lives affect our present one. It is also the example of the computer network I spoke about above, where a virus on one workstation can infect the central server and other stations. This was proof of what Dr. José Luis Cabouli maintains; for the spirit, time does not exist and the past is not really past because it is with us all the time.

The Egyptian Tarot

During the time I frequently visited Lito, whom I mentioned a few pages above as one of the support points on my path, I expressed my interest in learning to read the Egyptian tarot. He agreed. In those days, I could see how he was using it, as a tool to help others, to guide them, and not necessarily to predict their future. I remember that the first things that caught my attention in his deck were the archetypes with Egyptian motifs, a culture that has always fascinated me.

Lito's teaching method was not based on memorizing the meaning of each card, but on the idea that came to mind at that moment, as a sort of channeling. By putting a few cards together on the table, they conveyed a story, a message about the client in front of us. A card could mean one thing to one person, and something totally different to another. This allowed the reading to be very flexible.

Without realizing it then, today I understand it that way. We were channeling messages from another dimension. The informant could be our spirit guide, or the client's; or perhaps it was our Higher Self that manifested itself through the tarot. When I read the cards, I could feel the energy flow and the thoughts that I enunciated came to my mind as I saw each card or all of them together.

Over time, my readings got better and better. People were surprised at how detailed I could be, but the truth is that, little by little, I became disillusioned with them, as I saw that people came to me with superfluous motives and questions that had nothing to do with their spiritual evolution. Each reading was like taking an x-ray of the spirit of the client and understanding his or her true essence, and the situation he or she was going through. In other words, it was like taking off the mask they were wearing and discovering who they really were.

While it is true that my intention was always to help and guide others through tarot, and although I had managed to do so with a few, I realized that it was not the tool for me. It was not the way I wanted to do that work.

I have to admit that learning to read the Egyptian tarot helped me to develop a better perception beyond the five senses. After some time practicing, I noticed that it was easy for me to decipher the messages hidden between the lines. The words my clients said gave me the clue that would help me bring them to the origin of the symptom. I learned to detect the channel of communication that my client's subconscious used to communicate with me, giving me signals and messages that helped me get to the root cause of their symptom. This, in turn, gave me the tools to understand the patterns of behavior they carried with them from life to life.

During hypnosis education, as one begins to facilitate sessions, we usually focus on evaluating whether or not we are doing things right, whether we are using inductions correctly, whether the client is in a deep or light trance, or whether we are applying each technique correctly. As we gain more experience, everything that is done in a session begins to occur almost instinctively and automatically. That is when we begin to notice a series of additional events that occur during the session. The secret is to learn to open our mind and heart so that our guides - the hypnotherapist's and the client's - work through us. As Michael Newton says in his book, "Life Between Lives," the best therapist for a client is not us, but their spirit guide.

I noticed that I was comfortable with the technique when I started asking questions I normally would not have asked, saying things that were exactly what the client needed to hear, knowing what was going to happen next before the client finished explaining to me what he was seeing in a trance, using words that were not part of my vocabulary, but that meant everything to my client at that moment. In other words, I realized that I was channeling, receiving assistance from beings of light to help my clients in the best way possible. Although at first I used to say that I did not understand where those questions were coming from, today I not only understand, but I even ask for help and have mental consultations with those beings during my sessions so that they can guide me every step of the way.

My Information Technology Career

By the end of 2006, I was able to get a job at a corporation dedicated payroll processing and everything related to human resources nationwide in the United States. It was the first time I had worked for a company of that size. I was a Systems Analyst IV, which consisted of providing support for the different platforms offered to clients to process payroll and handle all aspects related to human resources. There were several platforms and my department dealt with large and important companies with a presence in several states and in other countries. We did not deal directly with the employees, but with the human resources managers and their information technology team.

The support was basically by phone and with remote connection to their computers and servers over the Internet. For those who are not familiar with the way an IT department works, you might understand that they are very cautious about who they allow to connect to their servers, what systems they install on them, and about following the suggestions provided by our team. One of the big issues in this type of environment is the ego; who knows the most, who is right, and above all, who is in charge.

When it was my turn to call a client to work on their case, they had basically already spent at least half an hour with the customer service team, maybe another half hour with the first level technical support team, where they had most likely been told that their case had to be escalated to the second level support team, my area. By the time I called the customer, they were usually pretty upset and desperate about the problems they were having with the platform, the time they had waited on hold, and the frustration that the other two teams had been unable to solve the problem.

During the first few months, seeing the way some users reacted, I thought they were upset with me, making my ego feel hurt and putting me on the defensive. This made communication not flow as well as it should, and it took me a while to establish rapport, a relationship of trust with the client, so that I could solve their problem.

This job taught me to put my ego aside, to empathize with the person on the other end of the call, and to understand how frustrated they could be. I learned to put myself in their shoes and let them know that I recognized how they felt and that I would feel exactly the same way if I were in their situation, but that if they would just allow me a few minutes, I could solve the problem.

I was able to talk to people with different levels of education, cultural backgrounds, people who spoke English and Spanish. Little by little, I developed the ability to connect with my client and then empathize, establish a relationship of trust - known as rapport exercises in hypnosis - and thus get them to work with me and let me guide them.

Since the communication was via telephone, I depended totally on my voice, its tone, cadence, and calmness, to achieve the desired effect in order to begin the process. In other words, the position I held for twelve years had helped me develop my hypnotic voice, that calm and gentle voice that transmits confidence. This is a fundamental tool for the practice of hypnosis.

Today, I do the same with my clients, starting with our initial interview. Without them noticing, and while they tell me about the events in their lives, I am adjusting my tone of voice, to gradually bring them to the state I need them in to start working with them. I empathize, establishing a relationship of trust by finding common aspects with those who can identify with me, and thus prepare their subconscious to begin to accept my suggestions, even before starting the induction.

SIGNALS AND MESSAGES

I remember the paragraphs from the book, "Many Lives Many Masters," by Brian Weiss, where he narrates how he began to receive messages through Catherine - the name he assigned to his patient - while she was in a trance. What caught my attention was the author's surprise while receiving all that information.

Just like Weiss, I would not be the exception for these kinds of events, these emotions. Long before I started practicing hypnosis, different psychics had told me what was coming for me in the future, but either they could not explain well what they were seeing, or I did not yet have the understanding necessary to process what they were revealing to me. I remember that I was always told that I would have to travel a lot. During the Egyptian tarot reading, Lito had already mentioned to me that in this reincarnation I had a special mission. My aunt Sonia, on the other hand, had told me in her tarot readings that I would also travel a lot. Up to that moment and at that age, what I had been told sounded interesting and mysterious, but as the years went by, I began to forget about those predictions.

It wasn't until 2014, while I was learning about regressive hypnosis, that the messages began to come again through my clients in a trance, especially those who didn't remember anything they had said in that state. These messages were also coming to me through other mediums, and while I decided at first not to give it too much thought, I came to a point where I simply could not ignore them any longer.

When I look back and remember every situation I was in, I realize that I was never alone, that I was always guided by my spirit guides and beings of light, not to deviate from my path until the day I could align myself with my purpose one hundred percent. The messages were not always pretty. There were times when my guides also let me know when I was going wrong and recommended that I change and view certain circumstances from another perspective. You could say that, on some occasions, I received a slap on the wrist from these beings of light. In order for you to better understand me, I would like to mention some of them.

Blair Styra

Blair, of Canadian origin and resident of New Zealand, is a medium who channels a spirit guide called Tabaash, who lived in ancient Sumeria. In 2014, Alba Weinman told me about her participation in an event with Dolores Cannon, where Tabaash gave personalized advice to all attendees, including her.

Alba had had a session with Blair, and had been surprised by what Tabaash had told her. She said she didn't need to say anything and that Tabaash talked to her about things she hadn't told anyone. Soon I was also encouraged to have a session with Blair.

A few months later I decided to contact Blair. After giving me a brief explanation about Tabaash and how he worked, Blair proceeded to put himself in the trance-like state necessary for Tabaash to use his body to communicate with me. Soon after, the wise spirit greeted me and began giving me a personalized coaching session. It was as if he knew everything about my life, mentioning various key points and situations that I had gone through, explaining the reason why.

Everything he mentioned was true and I was more than surprised as I listened to him.

During our second session in 2015, while Tabaash was talking to me, he suddenly turned his head to one side as if there was someone next to him and started talking to that invisible being in a language that I guess was the one he used in his life in Sumeria. After a few seconds he turned to see me and said, "Your guides are asking me to tell you that you should start practicing your presentation skills because we see you talking in front of many people in the future. Start preparing yourself." Although I had contemplated the idea of teaching hypnosis in the future, I had not seen or felt it as some sort of mission that I had been given, and if at any time I thought about doing demonstrations, I saw that as far off yet.

Tabaash couldn't have been more accurate with what he had told me in that session. A year later, I would begin teaching the Introspective Hypnosis technique to a small group that had formed on its own, with participants from North Carolina, Miami, Las Vegas and New Jersey. I taught that class in my living room for one weekend, and since that day, four years have passed in which I have been teaching it.

Little by little, the technique became known and, when I started teaching the live course online, Alba recommended it on her social media channels. That's how people from other countries could be registered to take it too. It was something extraordinary for me. It wasn't until September, 2018, that I invited Alba to collaborate with me in teaching a live class in Charlotte, North Carolina. I remember that 42 people attended from different states and even from abroad. That class would be the one that would change my life and my family's completely.

During the demonstration session on the penultimate day of the class, Belen, who had volunteered, was able to heal herself from fibromyalgia in front of everyone in attendance. Belen did not remember anything that happened in her one-and-a-half-hour session, and even thought that we had not even started yet. The root cause of Belen's symptom lay in a repressed emotion associated with a memory of her adolescence. It was an enriching experience for me.

Justine Alessi

By the end of 2017, one of my Facebook contacts was recommending tarot readings with Justine Alessi, a great friend of Dolores Cannon, who in turn helped her publish her book, "Rebirth of the Oracle." Justine had a reputation for being very accurate and, due to the uncertainty of the changes that were taking place in the company I worked for, I decided to schedule a reading with her.

Justine began her reading by saying many accurate things about my past and present. She told me that she saw in me a natural born teacher and that is why I had come to this reincarnation, to share knowledge. She went on to say that she was getting the traveler's card and that I would be traveling a lot in the future to teach. When I asked about my work situation, she told me that she didn't see me working for the company I was with for much longer, but she also said that they weren't going to let me go me because, even though they were letting others go, they needed me because I was bilingual. She saw that I was going to resign.

At that time, this didn't make sense to me, because the truth was that I was worried about my job stability as a systems engineer. While it was true that she saw me practicing hypnosis full time in the future, I felt that the time had not yet come. As the months went by, I saw the company continue to make changes and negotiate the departure of those who had several years of service and who earned the highest salaries. Little by little, my teammates were being let go, and everyone else was living with great uncertainty, as if waiting for the guillotine to fall on us.

Something inside me was telling me that I was fighting my destiny, that there were other more meaningful things I had to do, and that swimming against the current was becoming painful. I remember that, at that time, I began to suffer from migraines, problems with my urinary system, back pain, and high blood pressure. It was then that I started the Introspective Hypnosis course, in September, 2018, which I mentioned above. Upon completion of the course, I realized how important it was to share knowledge and help others heal. Once the class, which I had taught during one of my vacation weeks, was over, and as I sat at the computer to begin my daily work, I realized that I could no longer fight the current. That day, thanks to Catherine and Alba's insistence, I made the decision to resign during the first week of December of the same year.

Thus, my family went from working for twelve years for a company in exchange for a check that covered our expenses, to the alignment with our purpose; to not feeling that what we were doing was working; to not thinking about a budget. Money was never the motivation for my therapies or classes. The universe simply took care of us while we were doing what we came here to do: transmitting knowledge through love and forgiveness.

So, a year after my reading with Justine, everything happened just as she had predicted and I was able to start aligning myself with my purpose. From that day on, my symptoms disappeared completely. As we began 2019, Catherine, Alba, and I planned the classes that would be held both in the United States and in other countries. In that year, we visited the United Kingdom, the Netherlands, and Denmark. By 2020, classes were scheduled in France, the United States, Mexico, Australia and the Netherlands again. All the messages I had been receiving were beginning to come true, and I could not have been happier about what I was experiencing.

Dodris

One thing I have not stopped doing since I entered the world of hypnosis, is constantly updating myself through learning new techniques. I am convinced that, in this field, it is as important to be humble and to know how to ask for help or advice when needed.

It is important to recognize that there are other professionals with more years of experience and additional processes whom we must learn from.

As I mentioned a few pages ago, in October of 2019, at the suggestion of my friend and colleague, Genoveva Calleja, I decided to submit my resume for participation in the Life Between Lives technique course by Dr. Michael Newton. The course took place in a retreat center located in Maryland, United States, and lasted six days.

Something that the trainers frequently commented on was the fact that we were several Hispanics in the class, which was taught in English. We were seven of a group of twelve people. Such was the effort to get the material and concepts understood by everyone that they brought in a bilingual trainer as support.

To take this class, you had to fulfill a series of requirements, such as already knowing hypnosis and having tangible experience in regression to past lives. It was also necessary to verify the number of hours of training that each of us had. This meant that everyone in that course had the required experience and only came to learn a new hypnosis technique.

During the course of the class, and as is usually the case in most of these types of internship events, we would meet after class to talk, exchange experiences, or simply practice what we had learned. It was then that one of my classmates asked me to help her find the origin of a symptom she had, using Introspective Hypnosis. When I started the induction, I noticed that she went into a trance very quickly and that she was going into a very deep trance. During those minutes, we were able to find the root cause of that physical symptom and work on it.

Once she came out of the trance and we finished the session, I thought of asking her if she wanted to try to channel; that is, allow a spirit to use her body to communicate through it. I remember that after I made that suggestion, I was left wondering why I had done it since it is not common for me to go around asking something like that. My colleague agreed to try it in front of our other colleagues. As hypnosis is cumulative, this time she entered more quickly into a trance and we began to work. Using a visualization technique, I took her to a beautiful garden where I asked her to imagine a bench where she could sit and rest while I guided her towards the activation of her third eye, while touching her forehead. This way, she could see spirits both in that garden and in the room where we were.

> **Antonio**: Look around and tell me if there is a spirit in that garden where you are or in this room where we are.

> **Colleague**: There is one here.

> **A**: Look at the color of its energy and tell me what color it is.

> **C**: It's purple.

Immediately, I knew it wasn't a lost soul. As I said earlier, and as Michael Newton reported in his book, "Life between lives," purple indicates that the spirit is advanced. We could say that, starting with the color white and ending with purple, the darker the energy, the more evolved the spirit is.

> **A**: Describe how it presents itself to you.

> **C**: It presents itself as a black-skinned man in rags, as if he were a slave.

> **A**: Would you like to lend him your body to communicate with us or would you prefer that I ask him questions and you repeat what he says to you?

> **C**: I want to lend him my body so that he can communicate.

> **A**: I understand. I will count from three to one and when I reach one, you make the connection. Three, two...

I hadn't reached number one when my partner's head started to fall to one side and her whole body also leaned, as if she had lost control of it. I approached to hold her and keep her from falling, but at that moment the spirit took control and regained balance.

Antonio: Brother, we have already made the connection. You can communicate now.

Spirit: I'm happy to see you all together! I'm happy to see you here. I want to see you! I want to see you! -he said with a voice of happiness and enthusiasm, as if he were a friend who was seeing us after a long time.

A: If you know how to channel with your eyes open, then go ahead and, without finishing telling him that, he opened his eyes.

S: I am happy to see you all together. We have had to overcome many obstacles to bring you all together.

A: Excuse me, brother, do you know us?

S: Yes -he nodded.

A: From where?

He pointed his index finger upwards, giving us to understand that we knew each other from the spirit world, from when we were spirits before we reincarnated.

A: What is your name, brother?

S: Dodris, -he replied - each of you has been carefully chosen. You represent a continent that has suffered much. Each one of you is a link in a chain and it is not so much what you can do individually, but what you can do as a group. I suffered a lot too.

A: What year did you live in, brother?

S: For the fifteen hundred -it seemed to have been a slave.

We were perplexed by this communication. This not only validated the comments the trainers had made about having so many Hispanics together in the same group, which had never happened before, but it also validated what I had felt all this time and what I had been told by psychics, trance clients, and even Lito, when he told me of a special role in this reincarnation. This also confirmed what we had come to do in this life and my feeling of being in alignment with my purpose.

Dodris continued with the communication for a few more minutes. Because of the training I had, I decided to check out the kind of spirit we were communicating with, and asked him if he had the gift of telepathy, the ability to read our thoughts. He answered that he did. I proceeded to ask each of my colleagues present to ask him a mental question so that he could answer them. This is what happened: Dodris answered each of the questions asked, giving an explanation.

We were amazed. I had been able to talk to spirits before, but this communication had been different. This was an evolved being of light who knew us from the spirit world and who came to confirm the role we had played in this reincarnation.

Once Dodris disconnected from my colleague's body and I got her out of the trance she was in, we all looked at each other trying to understand what had just happened and, above all, to discover what we were going to do with that information.

Although each of us continued on our journey after that day, we are always in touch and know that, sooner or later, the time will come for us to collaborate as a group.

CLOSING THE CYCLE WITH MY FATHER

From the day I began writing this book, I watched the months go by as I progressed a few pages at a time, making sure my energy was in balance as I chose each word. In early 2020, I began to spend more time on it in an effort to finish it as soon as possible, but for some reason, I felt that, if I finished it then, it would not be complete.

During one of my conversations with Victoria, the young woman with psychic abilities with whom I had developed a friendship and mentoring role, I told her of my interest in finishing the book soon. I remember her interrupting me by saying that the spirit guides were communicating to her that the book was not important at the time and that there were other things I needed to take care of. It was for that reason, hearing the guides' message, that I focused on my courses and sessions with my clients.

By the end of 2019, I had seen my father's health break down. He had fought cancer for twelve years and had also suffered a heart attack from which he had miraculously been saved. In early 2020, I witnessed his rapid weight loss and how he began to walk more slowly. The end was near and I felt it was my duty to help my father in his transition; to guide him in his preparation, to understand what was going to happen, and how he should take it.

During his last three years of life, after distancing himself from me by divorcing my mother and starting a new family, my father and I were able to re-establish communication, which allowed us to work on issues we had pending. On the other hand, during those three years, my father also closed unfinished chapters with other members of our family. The soul always returns to the light when it is ready, and when it has completed what it came to learn in this reincarnation. That was the case with my father. I could see how, and perhaps unknowingly, he was putting an end to the chapters of his life.

On his last visit to the oncologist, in which I accompanied him, he was informed that the cancer was advanced and that, if he did not follow a chemotherapy treatment, he would only have three months to live. But if he followed it, there was a fifty percent chance that he could live two more years. Something told me that would not be the case. My father began the first session of chemotherapy, but after a few days he became weaker and almost stopped walking. His kidneys began to fail, making him sleepy most of the day, with small episodes of lucidity.

As I watched my father's health decline, something told me that I should be the one to stand by his side to help him transcend when the time came. Once again, my intuition did not fail. For the last three weeks, I spent almost every day with him, and for the last three days, I chose to stay at his house. On June 24, 2020, he died at home at the age of seventy-seven, accompanied by his family.

When my father took his last breath, while my mother, uncles and brothers were overwhelmed with sadness, I focused on helping him get out of his body. I talked to him, caressed his chest and promised him that everything would be okay, as he opened his eyes for the last time. This is an experience that I will always carry with me in my heart.

Although for a long time I thought I would be ready for this moment, I was not. My father was my first teacher. From him, I learned many things, such as the importance of having willpower, never giving up, and to love our family. In the face of life's adversities, my father always used to say that he would die next to the cannon, like soldiers do. And so he did, fighting until the last minute without giving up.

While it is true that our relationship had its ups and downs, everything happened as it was supposed to between us. This planet is a school where we come to learn and experience all kinds of emotions. My father played the role of a teacher, who came to teach me what life is all about through joy, sadness, anger, resentment, forgiveness, and finally, irreparable loss. The cycle of learning with my father was over.

From that episode, I understood why the spirits sent me that message with Victoria. The book, at that moment, was not something primordial. The most important thing was to spend time with my father and help him get ready for his departure. A few days after his death and having processed my emotions, I felt it was time to continue my writing.

HYPNOSIS IN THE NEW NORMAL

The year 2020 will be remembered as one of the most tragic years in the history of humanity, as it was the year in which the coronavirus (COVID-19) took thousands of lives and forever transformed the way we humans relate to each other. This book was completed during the global pandemic.

In the month of March of this same year, my wife Catherine, my children Tony and Christian, and Amy, his girlfriend, as well as my great friend Alba Weinman, the renowned medium Blair Styra, and about thirty other people who follow the Introspective Hypnosis technique, were in Peru, the country where I was born.

A year and a half ago I had begun to feel a great desire to take all those who practiced my hypnosis method or who resonated with what I was doing to Peru, specifically, to Cusco, capital of the ancient Inca empire. I could not define the need I felt to organize this trip, but I decided to let myself be guided by my intuition, which up to now had served as a compass. It had been a long time since I traveled through Cusco for the first and last time, when I was eighteen years old. That is why, in the middle of 2019, I decided to visit Cusco by myself in order to establish the places that would be on our itinerary, and the hotel where we would be staying, and to contact some locals to ask for their guidance.

While many might take this trip as a tourist, the truth is that, deep down, I felt there was another, bigger reason why we had to be there in March 2020. This trip had to be different, with a spiritual orientation. My plan was not to offer the standard tour that you get on the Internet, but one that looks at an expedition within us with the goal of knowing ourselves better and recognizing ourselves as a group.

When I arrived in Cusco, the city enveloped me again with its magic and energy, just as it did when I was a young man. Now, you could see more buildings and tourists. The streets were full of people and you could feel an atmosphere of joy and good vibes in the restaurants, bars and other stores around the main square.

On that first trip, I dedicated myself to taking pictures and recording videos to promote the trip. Also, I was able to meet with Gina and Stephanie, colleagues and friends who lived there, who guided me and helped me at all times.

When the day came to leave for Machu Picchu, I boarded the tourist train where destiny would conspire to have me meet Hector, a tourist guide with many years of experience, who was to sit next to me during the trip. We quickly struck up a conversation and I told him about my plan. Soon after, we had exchanged phone numbers for him to guide the March tour. He accepted and, to my surprise, invited me to join his group that day, since I did not have a guide.

Back in the United States, I told Catherine what had happened and she could see my enthusiasm in talking about this project. If I formed a group of ten people, I would consider the tour a success. Hector even warned me that it would take me a while to get everyone together, but I felt positive anyway.

When I told Alba about my experience and showed her the photos and videos, she immediately felt encouraged to join this adventure. Alba, who was born in Cuba, had immigrated to the United States at the age of three. For her, going to South America was completely out of her comfort zone, but she still decided to do it. At that time, she was in New Zealand staying at the home of psychic Blair Styra, whom I spoke about earlier. Without much thought, Blair also decided joined the trip. We were already three people.

Alba, Blair and I recorded a video for YouTube promoting the trip. Within days of the release, I had people who had paid the full cost months before our departure. Little by little, the group grew from ten to a total of thirty-seven people registered, at which point we had to close the registration to avoid to logistical issues.

The vast majority of those who registered were people who had taken my course in different countries. We had participants from the United States, Puerto Rico, Australia, Canada, England, Spain, Lithuania, Peru, New Zealand, Romania and Austria.

In the month of March 2020, we all left for Peru. Some only knew each other through our social media groups and others had taken the course together, but somehow or other, the connection was there.

The arrival in Cusco was magical. The face of amazement and joy that all the participants had was priceless. It didn't take long for them to feel comfortable and start connecting with each other. During an event that Blair and Alba organized for the first day in Cusco, different group exercises were done that helped not only to greater integration, but also to establish our intention in this new adventure. Blair channeled Tabaash, who told us that we had all come together again to receive something that we would carry with us for the rest of our lives. He also informed us that it would be our spiritual rebirth, in which none of us would ever be the same again. Tabaash could not have been more accurate.

Over the course of the next few days, some of the group began to enhance their psychic abilities. Jill, who had traveled all the way from New Zealand, would go into an almost uncontrollable trance when visiting certain archaeological sites, channeling spirits of light.

The same happened with Marisel, who further developed her ability to spontaneously channel light beings in any energetic place we visited.

Alba had already told me that, in a private session with Blair as soon as they arrived in Cusco, Tabaash had told her that she was going to undergo a great transformation, a kind of rebirth. He even told her that after the experience in the Inca city, my psychic abilities would be strengthened. And, they were. After that trip, I began to feel another kind of connection with my clients during my sessions. As they told me about the events they had experienced in this reincarnation or others, questions and words suddenly came to my mind without me knowing their origin. I had already been experiencing something similar, but this time it was different.

I began to have a more open connection with the subtle dimensions and to be more aware of the help I was receiving from the other plane to assist my clients. I was sure those questions, whose origins I didn't understand, were from my spiritual guide or theirs. My energy definitely changed, as did the style and approach in my sessions.

During an offering to the *Pachamama* -Mother Earth in Quechua- facilitated by Carlos Jorge Illapuma, *paqo* -an Andean priest from Cusco- some began to have metaphysical experiences. Sabrina, who traveled from the United States, entered into a deep trance during which she was assisted in healing the symptoms she had.

No matter where we went, something always took place, or else Blair was channeling beings of light, giving us messages of love and assisting us in our journey.

On the last day, when we went to Machu Picchu, Blair was guided to do a channeling of a being of light for the group, as a closure of our experience in the same citadel. I will now transcribe part of what I recorded on that occasion:

This is a very sacred place. A long time ago you were here and, in this life, you felt a call to return to it. It was not to regain something, nor to become something, but to remember everything.

"On the final day of this journey, where you have been together as a group, you are in the center of your heart. You have all loved each other, healed each other, remembered each other, and supported each other. You have stepped out of the world for a moment to live in this one, which is not complicated, nor is it filled with the life you normally have. You have also allowed yourselves to walk into yourselves. Now, the Self is greater than what you left at home, than your jobs and your families.

It is important to remember that you must learn to step out of your life sometimes, even for five minutes. This does not mean that you have to go on big excursions all the time, but that you have to know how to separate yourself from your life for a moment so that you remember where you are. What matters is where you are, not where you are going. It does not matter where you have been either, but where you are standing now, because where you are is really you.

So, in this moment, you are going to claim your holiness. I wish that in your thoughts you would put the intention of how you will choose to be from today. Pay attention to your feelings and ideas. It can be simple, or it can be great. Pay attention to it. Paying attention is very important because it will allow you to be the guide of your energies…"

At the end of this small ceremony that lasted almost an hour, the light being that communicated through Blair in a trance-like state, warned us that each of us would return to our countries and face difficult times, but that we had to be united. Now I understand that he was referring to the pandemic of COVID-19.

Everything I had felt when the idea of taking a group to Peru came to me, had materialized and been fulfilled. I felt honored to have been used as an instrument for this.

From that day on, none of us have been the same. We all changed in some way or another on an emotional, spiritual and psychic level. In the months that followed, we each began to develop certain skills that we didn't know we had, which would impact our practice of regressive and spiritual hypnosis.

We never imagined that, once our adventure in Cusco was over, our lives would change forever. When we left the Inca city behind, the president of Peru ordered the borders to be closed and six of us found ourselves unable to leave, thus complying with a nationwide quarantine. We spent the next ten days in social isolation in a rented apartment, being able to go out only to buy food and medicine. The streets were empty, the few people who circulated were forced to wear masks, there were no cars on the streets, and overnight, Lima and other cities in Peru had become ghost towns.

On the tenth day, when we were able to return to the United States on a humanitarian flight, we were surprised to find Miami's airport almost empty due to fear of the spread of the virus. How could the world change so quickly? How did we not realize that this was coming?

In the United States, the number of infected people increased rapidly. Supermarkets reduced their hours, companies sent their employees to work from home, schools closed, and restaurants, gyms and other places with a concentration of people were closed. Within a few months, the world order had changed completely. Suddenly, people were forced to stay in their homes.

In terms of practicing and teaching hypnosis, the virus also affected the way we help our clients through sessions. Although I was already teaching courses and facilitating live sessions over the Internet, I thought the number of clients would decrease dramatically. To my surprise, this was not the case. The number of scheduled appointments began to increase rapidly, as did the number of people registering for the online courses.

From a therapeutic point of view, quarantine and social isolation have forced humans to spend more time alone with themselves. It has given them the opportunity to self-analyze, and to face their fears. They have been forced to deal with those they had been avoiding while taking refuge in work, routine, and being constantly busy, not thinking or acting.

It has been a time when many people have needed help and guidance as they became introspective and understood the purpose of their circumstances. This could be the reason why the hypnosis sessions increased, but this would only be a guess.

Not only has the planet had a break from the daily activities of the big cities, but human beings have begun to understand the importance of interpersonal relationships. Something that had been taken for granted was now seen as part of a longed-for memory: meetings with friends and family, attending sporting events, or simply going to a restaurant to eat.

In addition, we have gone through a new awakening of consciousness, understanding that our freedom ends where the rights of the other begins. We are learning that, to beat this virus, we have had to learn to take care of each other.

Why would we have chosen to reincarnate in these difficult times? It is at this point that all spiritual volunteers of all orders come into action, bringing a message of love, hope and compassion.

I always wonder why the trip to Cusco took place just at the time when the world was beginning to close its borders and the world order was changing. Coincidence? I don't think so. Perhaps we had to return to our homes spiritually stronger than ever, to help our clients, to help our own, and to help ourselves.

CONCLUSIONS AND ACKNOWLEDGEMENTS

Today I look at the path I have traveled and realize that I am not the same person I was when I started the practice of regressive hypnosis. When I analyze the past, I can see that, at all times, I was preparing myself for what I would experience in the future. Every sad or happy event in my life, every person put on my path at different times and levels of evolution, every technique learned, every message received through psychics and my trance clients, and every client sent to my door, had a purpose.

Today I write these lines out of gratitude to the universe and to the beings of light who have assisted me throughout this adventure, which still continues. I also thank my clients, because from each one, I was able to learn a new concept that I have then shared with others, to assist them in their passage on Earth; because through their healing, I was also allowed to heal my own wounds.

I write this with total gratitude to my wife Catherine and my children Antonio, Christian and Sebastian. This is for their love, patience and support in all that we have experienced together. Without their help, I would not be who I am now or where I am today.

I also thank my parents Antonio and Rosa María, my brothers, Vitor, Gianfranco, and Francesco, because I learned a lot from each of them, whether through sad or happy situations. To my cousin Juan, who played the role of the older brother during the first years of my childhood until the beginning of my youth.

I also thank my friends and colleagues, Alba Weinman and Genoveva Calleja, for having shared this path of learning and spiritual evolution together. To Aurelio Mejía, whose wisdom, simplicity, and generosity, influenced my practice of hypnosis and my evolution as a human being. Today, I understand that we are spirits having a human experience and that, as spirits, we belong to a spiritual group, a kind of classroom. With those companions I am reincarnated from life to life learning together with them.

Today, sitting in front of my computer, I can say that I know that life is a play tailored to our spiritual evolution. In that play, we have a leading role, which in turn has other actors of our own choosing. With some we sign contracts, with others we acquire karma. Some will play the role of heroes, while others will play the role of villains, allowing us to learn through each of them, whether in love or in pain.

Today I also understand that we are not victims of life, nor of other people. Every sad, happy, or traumatic event was carefully planned by our spirit before reincarnation, because it knew what we had to learn. Even accidents are not accidents, for they have a purpose. Everything has an end. Everything is learning.

Now I know how fundamental it is to take responsibility for every event that touches us and will touch us. We must always ask ourselves the reason for each event. Why am I going through this? What should I learn from this circumstance? We cannot change what has already happened, but we can change our perception about the event, how we decide to live it or remember it. We have control over the emotion we choose to associate with it. For our spirit, there is only the now, and for our spirit, life is one and is experienced through various bodies. For that reason, the feelings and symptoms that can generate negative emotions, can follow us from reincarnation to reincarnation if we do not close that chapter.

Today I understand that the solution to any difficult situation that we have to live through, is not to run from it, forget it, or leave it aside. The correct approach is to embrace that experience and allow ourselves to process all the emotions it brings with it. We will learn more from these complicated scenarios than from any other, because they were planned by our spirit before we were born.

Today I understand that our evolution as spirits is achieved through love, forgiveness, and helping our fellow man; that our goal is to remember who we really are and why we are here; that once we remember, we must help others remember who they are too. It will always be beautiful to learn our lessons from love, but there are times when we must learn them from pain, which is only an amplifier of learning.

While the journey that Catherine, our children, and I decided to travel has been filled with much work and sacrifice, it has also been filled with joy and enormous satisfaction, as we helped others through the Introspective Hypnosis sessions and classes.

We have had the privilege of traveling, giving training courses, and teaching others how to help through hypnosis. But beyond the fascination of soaking up other cultures, I value having met wonderful and big-hearted people, eager to receive knowledge and start applying it. This feeling goes beyond our expectations. No matter where the course is scheduled, people are sent from different parts of the world to learn this technique.

In 2019, for example, we had to travel to New Zealand and Holland. I remember that, in the class I taught in this last destination for the end of the year, it was difficult for me to contain my emotions when I listened on the last day to each learning group facilitating sessions in their own language. As I walked among them, I heard the technique in Dutch, English, French, German and Finnish. I was witnessing, on a small scale, what this course meant and the scope it was going to have. I had been chosen to pass on knowledge, a technique based on love, forgiveness and hope, which was to be used in different languages, cultures and contexts. I never felt more honored by the role I had been given.

In January 2020, we went to France to teach the first class in English with simultaneous translation into French. Today, in the midst of this new normality due to the Covid-19 virus, I continue to help people heal through virtual hypnosis sessions. And I continue to teach what I know in the same way.

The messages from the spiritual world have not stopped being transmitted, both during the sessions with my clients, and in the courses given. The beings of light who assist us always take advantage of the trance of some of the participants to start a conversation. It is always a pleasure to witness this event.

Finally, I will be eternally grateful to my spiritual guides and beings of light for always being by my side when I needed them. Thank you for your help and for keeping me on the path I had to walk. I do not know what the future holds for me, although I can feel it. A new phase has begun for us.

MY SOUL'S
PURPOSE

MISSIONS, LESSONS AND PAST LIVES
THROUGH HYPNOTIC REGRESSION

Made in the USA
Coppell, TX
29 September 2022